EASY-TO-MAKE
COSTUMES
FOR STAGE AND SCHOOL

JULIA TOMPKINS

WITH DRAWINGS BY JOYCE ASSER

DIAGRAMS BY THE AUTHOR

Publishers PLAYS, INC. *Boston*

© J. Tompkins 1975

First American edition published by Plays, Inc. 1976

Published in Great Britain under the title
More Stage Costumes and How to Make Them

Library of Congress Cataloging in Publication Data

Tompkins, Julia.
  Easy-to-make costumes for stage and school.
  Includes index.
    1. Costume design. I. Title.
TT507.T6 1976   646.4'7   75-28277

ISBN 0-8238-0205-1

Printed in Great Britain

CONTENTS

ACKNOWLEDGEMENTS

I offer my most sincere and grateful thanks to the following who have all helped me so much in the completion of this book: to the editorial staff of Pitmans for their encouragement, patience and technical guidance at all times; to Joyce Asser for the delightful drawings of costumes and details, which so greatly enhance and clarify the text; to Violet Bibby for her careful scrutiny of the manuscript and of the diagrams; to Margaret Cobby for typing the manuscript and to Clive and Quinton Cobby for 'calling over' and checking; to the staff at Borough Road Library, Southwark, for obtaining books and patiently renewing them; to my husband, John Tompkins, for much help with the diagrams, and above all, for affording me the time to concentrate on the book, by doing all the time-consuming domestic chores.

INTRODUCTION

The analogy of the quart-into-a-pint-pot is nowhere more applicable than in the selection of material for any book on costume making. When I had finished *Stage Costumes and How to Make Them* I was conscious that although I had covered the broad outlines of each period of English costume from Saxon times to the present day, many variations had had to be dismissed rather summarily and the costumes of other countries and epochs were not discussed at all. The intention of this book is to draw in some of the latter under the broad headings of Egyptian, Biblical, Greek, Roman and Renaissance, and to enlarge upon ideas already presented, offering something a little more elaborate for the more adventurous. I have also included brief sections on Church vestments and American costume and on accessories, head wear and footwear (in as far as the latter can be contrived rather than hired or bought).

To make convincing costumes it is not necessary to be an expert on costume, nor is it necessary to know how the authentic garment was put together. For my designs I have undertaken no erudite research but have relied on reproductions of contemporary portraits. I have not used any material which is not easily available to anyone with access to a public library and I gratefully acknowledge my debt to those who have so assiduously tilled the ground and sown the seed in the fields from which I have culled.

All my patterns are based on a simple 'basic' pattern. Most makers of paper dress patterns include one of these, consisting of a plain bodice, a four-piece flared skirt and a straight 'shift'. A pyjama pattern serves excellently as a basic pattern for men's costumes.

When I start to make a costume, whether from a designer's drawings or from a portrait, I first of all analyse it in terms of present-day cutting methods, and break it down into basic sections. This preliminary dissection gives a rough idea of where to begin to adapt the pattern, and helps to make even the most

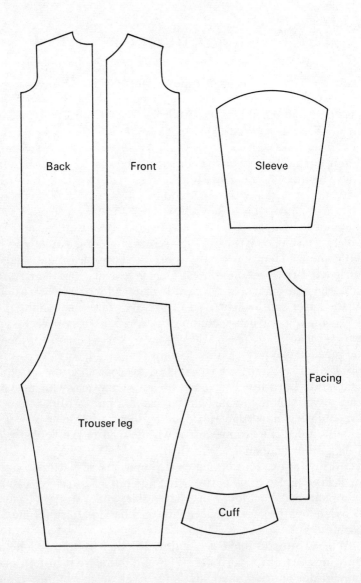

Figure 1   Basic pattern, male

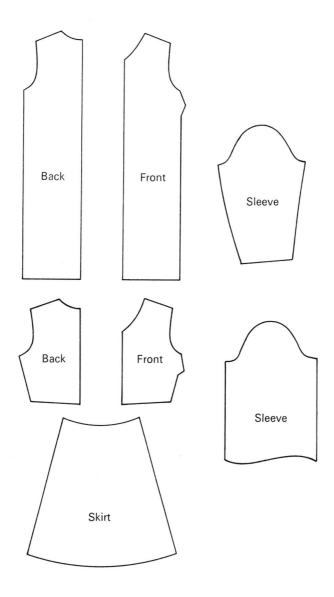

Figure 2   Basic pattern, female

complicated and elaborate costume seem possible.

Having decided on the component parts of the costume my method is then to cut a replica of the bought pattern. This I place on more newspaper and, having modified the outline as necessary, cut the pattern from which I am going to work. All the pattern diagrams in this book are based on this principle, showing the pieces of bought pattern (shaded) adapted, and, in some cases, positioned for cutting. The black continuous lines indicate cutting lines for modified patterns; those areas of the original pattern pieces which lie outside these lines can be discarded unless they are labelled otherwise. Gathering and slash lines are clearly indicated or explained in the text. Double material is shown by a small shaded portion at the corner of the diagram.

The patterns are based on a size 38 in chest for men and a 34 in bust for women. It is important to check the following measurements when cutting a costume to fit a particular individual:

Bust or chest

Waist

Hips

Shoulders

Across back (about half-way between shoulder and armpit)

Neck to waist (from the knob at the base of the neck to the natural waistline)

Arm (outer measurement from point of shoulder to waist—arm raised and bent).

This is a book for amateurs, by an amateur. What I offer is a practical and inexpensive way of achieving the authentic outline and dressing a production in such a way that the audience is *interested*.

CHAPTER ONE

EGYPTIAN

It is impossible to do more than generalize in such a vast field, so I offer merely a few suggestions for making some of the more familiar components of Egyptian costume. I must acknowledge the very great help that Margot Lister's book *Costume* affords in this respect. She provides a kind of distillation or *essence* of pictures and frescoes which in their original form are often difficult to interpret. Guidance on actual fabrics used—colours, jewels and accessories, arrangement of costumes etc.—is absolutely essential, and any wardrobe mistress who has to start from scratch would do well to badger her library for a copy of this indispensable book. I only wish it had been available in my own 'wardrobing' days.

Figure 3   Sphinx headdress

One of the Egyptian headdresses with which most people are familiar is that of the Sphinx. This was a royal headdress of linen, striped in blue and white. It should be made from fairly stiff linen, denim or even hessian (the latter would need to be painted to obtain the white stripes). Take the measurement from shoulder to shoulder across the top of the head—about 36 in (90 cm)—and cut a rectangle of material about 20 in (50 cm) wide. The stripes must run from back to front, that is, across the width.

Make a headband from leather, vinyl fabric or the like, about 2 in (5 cm) wide, and long enough to fit across the forehead to the ears—about 12 in (30 cm). Paint this strip in gold, and attach tapes at each end. Join to the centre 12 in (30 cm) on one of the long sides of the fabric. The front of the headband is ornamented with a snake emblem, also in gold. Tie tapes at the back, and allow the folds to fall on either side of the face.

Figures 4, 6 and 7 show three more easily contrived headdresses.

I

Figure 3   Sphinx headdress

Figures 4 and 5   Nefertiti headdress

The headdress is red, made either from leather or stiffened linen in the original, but could most easily be contrived from buckram covered with a red adhesive vinyl such as Contact or Fablon. Cut the buckram (or thin flexible card if only for one wearing) as in *figure 5*, allowing a 2 in (5 cm) surplus for the overlap—don't be tempted to skimp this otherwise it won't hold the cylindrical shape. Cut the vinyl, felt, linen, leather or whatever material is being used, allowing good turnings on all edges. If using contact vinyl, don't remove the backing paper until you are ready to stick the vinyl to the buckram.

Overlap the buckram and make sure that the head measurement is correct, allowing for the fact that, for comfort's sake, it is mounted on a small cap.

Tack the overlap with large zig-zag stitches. Buckram tends to 'fight', so a few turns of Scotch Tape help to keep it to the circle; and also it can be carefully steamed into shape, but great care must be taken in this operation, as steam burns are nasty. Allow a jet from a steaming kettle to play through the cylinder, but don't allow the buckram to become too limp. Remove from steam and while still warm, roll gently in both hands until cold. This will help to maintain the curve. When quite cold and *dry*, apply the vinyl. This is best done flat on a table. Peel back a few inches of the backing paper at the straight edge and fit the buckram at the overlap, smoothing out any wrinkles. Keep peeling off the paper, rolling the cylinder as you go, and continually smoothing, until all the paper is removed and the cylinder is covered. Snip the surplus along top and bottom

Figure 4   Nefertiti headdress

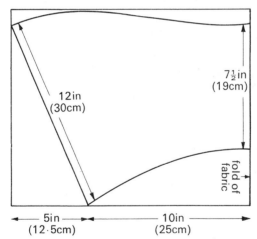

7½in
(19cm)

12in
(30cm)

fold of
fabric

← 5in → ← 10in →
(12·5cm)   (25cm)

Figure 5   Diagram for Nefertiti headdress

edges, turn inwards and press into position. It is not really necessary to fill in the top of the crown.

Make a tight-fitting skull cap with a front flange deep enough to turn back on to the crown. No hair must show beneath this headdress, so if the wearer has a lot of hair the cap must be deep enough for it all to be coiled and tucked inside. This

inner cap can be a straight strip to fit the wearer's head, about
$3\frac{1}{2}$ in (9 cm) wide finished width, with a $\frac{1}{2}$ in (1 cm) hem at the
top through which is threaded a tape or elastic, drawing up to
fit. It doesn't matter if it doesn't close completely—it will stop
the headdress from slipping down the forehead.

The decorated band can also be made from vinyl, in blue,
red, gold and white cut into squares and stuck in place as shown
in the drawing. The ornament in front, like that of the Sphinx
headdress, is in the form of a golden cobra.

If the headdress is made of non-stick fabric, make the buckram cylinder as before; cut the material to the same pattern
and stick it to the cylinder with a rubber cement such as
Copydex, overlapping the seam allowance as with the vinyl.
Snip the turning allowances and Copydex into place.

Figure 6   Medallion headdress

Figure 6   Medallion headdress

This woman's headdress consists of numerous strands of linked
medallions. Start by making a wire coronet to fit the crown of
the head. Then go begging for milk-bottle tops or yoghurt
tops. You will also need about two hundred thin curtain rings
or fine wire plant rings. Wash the bottle tops, smooth them out
carefully, and cover the rings to form medallions. Link these
together in tens, using fine florists' wire or fuse wire, and attach
to the circlet. The seven centre strands should, of course, be

proportionately shorter. Glue a diamanté stone in the centre of each medallion. Alternatively, sew buttons or medallions to narrow tinsel ribbon, used double.

Figures 7 and 8 Double crown of Egypt

This is the combined crowns of Upper and Lower Egypt. The inner, bottle-shaped section is white; the outer section is red. The first can be made of felt, and the second of contact vinyl on buckram, or also of felt, cut as in *figure 8*. It will be easier to make the red crown with the seam centre front. Cut the foundation in buckram, and cut two matching pieces in vinyl. Deal

Figure 7   Double crown of Egypt

with the inside first. Lay flat on a table and peel off the backing paper. Position the buckram and snip turning allowance on the curved edges. Pull back the vinyl from the centre front sufficiently to allow the overlapping of the buckram to the correct size. Hold firmly (get help if available!) and then stick the vinyl turnings down. The outer overlap will probably 'fight'. Hold it in place with a couple of spring clothes pegs or bulldog clips. (If a stapling gadget is handy, put a few staples in for firmness.) Press all turning allowances over the edges of the buckram and smooth into place. Lay the other piece of vinyl flat and peel away backing paper, then match up exactly at centre back, and smooth down all round, overlapping turnings centre front. Clip turnings on all curved edges, turn in and press into position. Trim with snake emblem and contrasting band, and fix to inner crown, which must fit closely. Oversew the two sections together and add a felt chin-strap. The feather is slotted under the band on the right side.

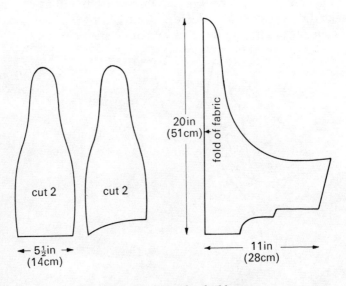

cut 2

cut 2

20in
(51cm)

fold of fabric

← 5½in →
(14cm)

← 11in →
(28cm)

Figure 8   Diagram for double crown

Figures 9 and 10 portray a pharaoh and his queen of about 1500 BC.

Figures 9 and 11   Pharaoh

The pharaoh's costume is simply a broad pleated loin cloth tied in front over a pleated apron with a brightly decorated hem. Fairly permanent pleats can be ironed into Terylene. The easiest way to do this is to pin firmly to an ironing board. First mark the pleats, then pin on to the board and press with a steam iron.

Figure 9   Egyptian pharaoh   *Figure 10   Egyptian queen*

This pharaoh's headdress seems to have been a war crown, made of stiffened linen or of leather, coloured blue. Cut as indicated in *figure 11* and join with a narrow seam, using a fairly loose tension, so that the seam can be flattened with the thumb nail.

Various accessories appertain to a pharaoh, such as the crook and the flail, and these are not difficult to contrive. Always, there is colour, vivid, bold, and sharply contrasted.

Figures 10 and 12   Egyptian queen

The queen wears a long pleated tunic which can be simply an

accordion-pleated tube of fine linen or nylon, gathered on to an elastic just above the bust line, and anchored to the wearer's bra straps. In actual fact, Egyptian styles preceded the topless fashions of this century by a few thousand years, and the original costume would have fitted tightly under the bust, held in place either by a single diagonal shoulder strap, or by straps passing over each shoulder, joined to the tunic between the breasts. Whether or not this style is used depends very much on the type and place of the actual stage production.

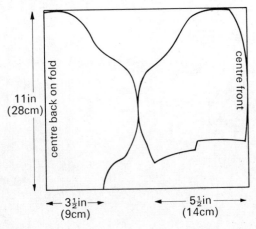

11in
(28cm)

centre back on fold

centre front

←─ 3½in ─→
(9cm)

←──── 5½in ────→
(14cm)

Figure 11   Diagram for pharaoh's war crown

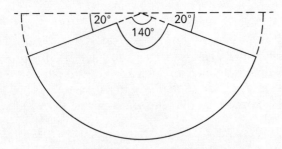

20°   140°   20°

Figure 12   Foundation for jewelled collar

Over the shoulders a wide transparent stole is gathered at the neck, under a deep jewelled collar. These circular collars are typical of Egyptian costume over a very long period, and must have been exceedingly beautiful, consisting of polished carnelian, lapis-lazuli, combined with green and red enamelled plates, and set in gold. Once again the humble milk/yoghurt top can be called into service, as well as coloured foil in various colours. Make a foundation collar (*figure 12*) in plain material— two thicknesses of cotton sheeting interlined with Vilene would make a good foundation. Cut cardboard or buckram segments in various shapes, cover neatly with coloured foil and stitch in rows to the collar. Touch in carefully with gold paint between the segments.

The queen's headdress is made in the same way as that already described for the Nefertiti headdress. The height may be varied as desired.

Figure 13   Vulture headdress

Another royal headdress was the vulture crown. Make a foundation skull cap in felt or esparterie. A firm foundation is necessary as this crown may have to be set in position while the wearer is on stage (Cleopatra's death scene for instance). It is a very stylized headdress, symbolic rather than imitative.

Cut a piece of buckram for the wings as shown in the diagram, and mark out into 'pinions'. Either gild the actual buckram, or use the metallic contact vinyl; stick this on the unmarked side. Cut along the marked lines to within 1 in (2 cm) of the edge and then steam buckram into an inverted 'U' shape.

Cut another piece of buckram as in *figure 13* for the body of the vulture, and mark into pinions; gild, or stick on Contact, and cut as before. Attach this section to the crown of the skull cap, then draw down the pinions so that they overlap and meet at the base of the cap. Anchor firmly, then bend the ends up into a fan, to represent the vulture's spread tail feathers. Make the vulture's head from felt (in the same way as a toy duck's head is made). A book on toymaking will explain this. Gild and decorate with diamanté eyes, and attach to the front of the skull cap. Cover the front of the crown with milk-top medallions, and attach the wings firmly across the crown of the skull cap. It is impossible to give exact measurements for this headdress, dimensions depend upon the size of the wearer's head and the type of production for which the headdress is required. However, the finished product should not be unmanageable.

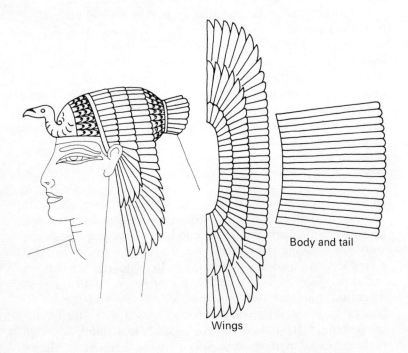

Body and tail

Wings

Figure 13   Vulture headdress

Strictly authentic wigs would be hot and unwieldy, and not particularly attractive. In these days of wig-wearing, however, it should not be difficult to find one which will blend in. The hair falls straight to the shoulders, and has a thick fringe across the forehead. With present-day hair styles it may even be that there is no need for wigs.

There is wide scope for ingenuity in this field. Girdles of medallions can be picked up cheaply; handicraft shops sell heavy gold chain by the yard. As an alternative to the medallions, the headdress in *figure 6* could be made from this chain.

Footwear was simple, and many sandals of Eastern type are now to be found on sale at quite low prices. Slaves went barefoot.

CHAPTER TWO

BIBLICAL

This chapter is concerned with making costumes suitable for biblical plays—nativity plays, miracle and mystery plays, plays set in Old Testament times. (Roman costume, which is more than likely to be needed in this context, is described in the next chapter.)

Drapery plays a large part, and so do robes and tunics which are not difficult to cut, the only real problem lies in anchoring them securely. Effects depend very much on the designer and producer's imaginative use of colour.

The loose robe can be utilized for practically any 'biblical' production, simply by varying the texture and richness of the material, and by evolving different trimmings. Made in a plain homespun fabric, it is suitable for the Shepherds and St Joseph; carried out in vivid colours, it is suitable for the Magi, who are not specified in the Gospel as belonging to any particular race, but are described as 'wise men from the east'. Angels also can be clothed in robes.

Sheeting suggests itself as a suitable material for most of these costumes, particularly Bolton twill which has a softer appearance, being unbleached. The snag with a twill weave is that it frays easily and seams must be either double or welted (that is, both edges pressed to one side and a further row of machine stitching run $\frac{1}{4}$ in from the seam). Use welted seams for the angels' wide sleeves and trim raw edges fairly close ($\frac{1}{8}$ in).

Figure 14 shows the way in which the basic pattern can be adapted for cutting a robe, but note that the layout shown for the sleeves can be used only with reversible fabric.

With the necessarily wide variation of sizes it is impossible to lay down hard and fast figures for quantities, but a rule-of-thumb method (which I give only in Imperial measurements) is to take the full length from back of neck to ground, double it and add $\frac{1}{2}$ yd of 36 in fabric. This will allow for the wide sleeves.

When using 72 in fabric halve the amount; with 54 in fabric allow the length from neck to ground and add $\frac{3}{4}$ yd.

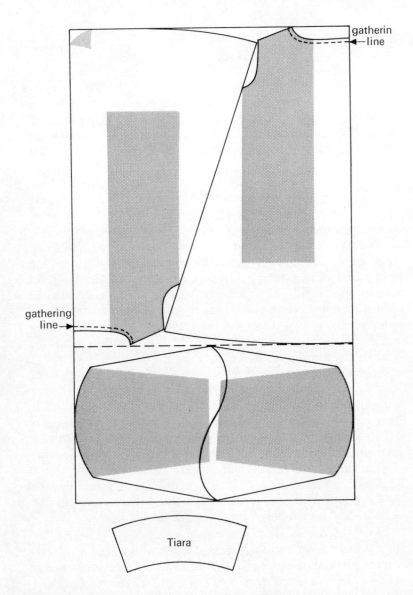

gathering
line

gathering
line

Tiara

Figure 14   Persian king's robe

Angels' robes, which might be cut slightly wider, will need the addition of a further ¼ yd in each case, that is ¾ yd instead of ½ yd of 36 in and 1 yd instead of ¾ yd with 54 in fabric. I feel it is very necessary to add a warning here that some materials such as winceyette, flannelette and cotton molleton, though suitable in texture, are potentially dangerous. Unless the retailer can guarantee that they are flameproof they must never be used without first being treated by soaking in a proofing solution: drip dry, do not wring out. It is easier to treat the whole length of material before cutting; by hanging it over the bath the residue of the solution can be used again for the next length.

The following formula was supplied by the Theatres Section of the Fire Service and has also been tested on various fabrics:

10 oz Borax and 8 oz Boracic Acid dissolved in
1 gallon water.

Quantities required will vary according to amount of fabric to be treated, but a gallon will treat about three yards.

Women's costumes do not seem to be so well documented as men's, but a steady diet of cinema and television biblical drama must have left recollections in the minds of most of us. Depending on the character to be depicted, costume can vary from simple and homespun, ample and flowing, to scanty and diaphanous. The former may consist of a plain full-length tunic in subdued colouring or white linen (cotton, nylon), with a cloak of heavier material, and a shawl head covering. More exotic robes can be made from brocade, on caftan lines, with diadems and jewels on the lines already described. For the Jezebels and Salomes: a jewelled bra and a see-through skirt over a bikini.

The Old Masters are not really much help here because they usually depicted biblical characters in their own contemporary costume. However, some of the plainer flowing gowns of the Renaissance would blend in without looking too out of place.

Figures 15 (a, b,) and 16   Assyrian King

The Assyrian king in the illustration wears a fringed scarf-like garment which was a long plain strip of fabric wound round the body skirt-wise and over the shoulders. Its predominant feature

Figure 15(a)   Assyrian king

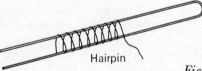

Hairpin

Figure 15(b)   'Hairpin' for fringe

is fringe, which was evidently very important. Fringe is expensive to buy, but again, with patience and ingenuity can be contrived. The easiest way is to cut a long narrow strip, machine this to the robe then snip it carefully into very narrow pieces. Alternatively, if you can find some old-fashioned chenille curtains, these make excellent fringe. (In fact many a curtain-maker in the past has probably ended up with fringe she didn't want, as chenille frays if you so much as look at it.) Cut strips double the depth of the fringe required, fold in half, and machine *raw* edges to the garment—this will leave the fringe-tails hanging in loops (*don't* cut them) and will prevent the raw ends from shedding the chenille. Snip the cotton warp and draw the threads.

Wool fringe can be machined straight on to the garment. Make a 'hairpin' of galvanized wire (about 12 gauge), giving the width needed (*figure 15b*). About 14 in (36 cm) is a manageable length. Wind rug wool or thick double-knit wool until the 'hairpin' is full. Machine along the edge close to inside arm pulling out the 'hairpin' and rewinding as the work proceeds. (There was in fact a gadget for making rugs on these lines called the Empire Rugmaker, but I cannot say whether it is still obtainable. It might, however, be worth enquiring at a handicraft or sewing machine shop.)

Another way of making fringe is on a knitting machine. Cast on a small number of stitches—equivalent to a cardigan welt. If a double-bed machine is available, so much the better, as this will make a heading which does not curl. Knit a few yards as required; machine to robe with at least three rows of stitching, then cut the free edge and pull the rows undone. Steam to get out the crinkles, and remember that the ultimate depth of the fringe will be about four times the original depth of the strip.

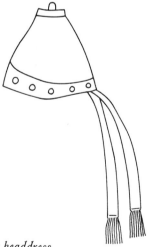

Figure 16   Diagram for Assyrian king's headdress

The Assyrian king wears a kind of mitre, in purple, banded with gold. Felt would be the most suitable material to use. An old hat crown can be steamed and stretched over a flower-pot then gently pulled to the requisite curve. Alternatively, the mitre can be cut from felt, as in *figure 16*, steamed and pulled into shape. Add a small felt knob on top, and fringed streamers at the back.

Figures 14 and 17   Persian king

Another kingly robe, which would not be out of place in a nativity play for one of the Magi.

Figure 17   Persian king

The cut of the gown is not complicated and can be made from the basic pattern, adapted as in *figure 14*. The hem and sleeves are decorated with vivid braid, and a necklace similar to that shown in the Egyptian chapter is added. The tiara is virtually an inverted flower-pot, and a flower-pot can in fact be used to make a pattern from which to cut it. Find one—plastic for preference—which fits the wearer's head. Take a double sheet of newspaper and wrap up the pot, tucking in the paper round the top. Cut round the creases made by the edges of the pot and trim off the overlap of paper round the wall of the pot so that the edges just meet.

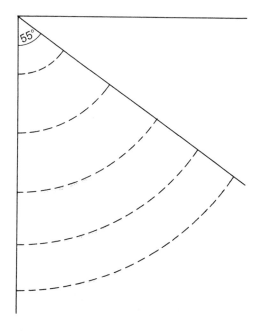

Figure 18   Segment of a circle with apex of 55°

The shape you have made in this way is in fact a segment of a circle with an apex of 55° (which can also of course be produced by mechanical means using a protractor). It is a shape which has innumerable uses in costume making as it can provide a template not only for all sorts of headgear (crowns and brims), but also, by extending the sides, for a flared skirt, a cape, a fishtail inset into a skirt, a train and curved pieces such as collars, basques and flounces (*figure 18*).

Angels' wings belong to the 'props' department, but making them can be so fraught with disaster that sometimes it is preferable to dispense with them and be content with haloes which can be made from buckram.

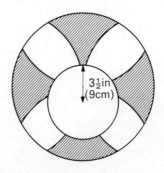

Figure 19   Halo for angel

Figure 19   Haloes

Take head measurement, divide by six and add ¼ in (0·5 cm). This gives the radius of the inner circle. Cut a circle of paper 14 in (36 cm) in diameter. (7 in radius using compasses, otherwise fold a piece of paper in four and mark 7 in (18 cm) from corner.) Fold in half and mark inner circle 2 in (5 cm) from outer edge, thus making the halo slightly narrower at the back, and so less likely to fidget the wearer. This gives a plain, firm-fitting halo. If it is still too tight, trim *sparingly*, otherwise it will fall about your ears. It is very important that measurements should be accurate; circles have a nasty habit of magnifying errors, and the nearest half-inch just will not do. Always remember that having cut, you can't put it back, so use the scissors sparingly. *Figure 19* shows the average measurement for the radius of the inner circle; it is not intended as an exact guide.

Cut the buckram all in one piece, and oversew a strand of millinery wire over the outer edge. This is one of the instances when *millinery* wire should be used. It is firm and strong and, because it is bought already wound, it will give a perfect circle. Overlap the ends slightly at centre back (the stitching will hold them), and cover with surgical plaster. For greater comfort, machine bias binding round the inner edge, and if the halo shows signs of slipping when worn, attach it to the top third of an 'Alice' band.

Gild with paint, or cover with gold paper in the form of a cross—as may be seen in paintings, or use gold satin and make up in the same way as the stephane in the Accessories chapter.

Figure 20   Crowns

Crowns for the Magi can also be made from buckram. The study of pictures and Christmas cards will suggest a variety of shapes, and again, simplicity is more effective. These were Oriental kings, in a pre-Christian era, and any shape remotely suggestive of Christianity, such as the later fleur-de-lis or cruciform trefoil, should be avoided.

Make templates in thin card and mark on buckram with ball-point pen. The width of the template should be $\frac{1}{6}$th of the head measurement. First draw half design on folded paper; cut and open out, then trace on to card. When cutting, allow an extra 1 in each end for overlap. *Figure 20* gives three suggested templates.

To achieve an outward curve, the points of the crown need to be wired. It is an unnecessary chore to stitch wire all round the edges. The same effect can be obtained by a straight piece of wire fixed to the inner side with Scotch Tape. The best kind of wire for this purpose is that used by florists for wiring bouquets. It comes in bundles of 9 in lengths and is obtainable from florists' sundriesmen. As an alternative, the paper-covered wire plant ties, from any gardening shop, will serve.

Paint and decorate flat. Decorations may be as elaborate as you can afford—strip diamanté, sequins, beads, anything that sparkles; and if it has to be strictly utility, ordinary buttons covered with sweet wrappings, milk-bottle tops or cooking foil will glitter bravely—to add some colour to the latter, cover them in turn with coloured cellophane film.

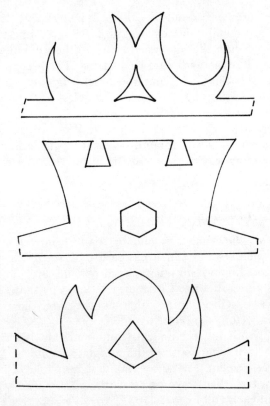

Figure 20   Crowns for the Magi : templates

Finally, join by overlapping the ends about 1 in to give a firm fit, and stitch each edge securely. Copydex a length of 1 in ribbon velvet round the lower inside edge to avoid scratching the wearer's forehead. Bend points gently to required curve.

CHAPTER THREE

GREEK AND ROMAN

In the minds of most of us, 'Greek-and-Roman' is a portmanteau term vaguely associated with old sheets and the Elgin Marbles. (To the wardrobe mistress, with her eye on a tight budget, it means yards of lovely material all in straight pieces, ready for the *next* production.) There's a bit more to it than that, however, and quite an amount of colour and interest can be introduced. Research has brought to light the fact that considerably more colour and decoration was used than would appear from the pallid marbles from which we take our idea of the period.

The basic garment of both men and women in ancient Greece was the 'chiton', a tunic in its simplest form, consisting of straight, rectangular pieces of material caught at the shoulders with a brooch, and held in place by a girdle. The effectiveness of this style lies entirely in the careful arrangement of the draping, and when this has been achieved, it should be firmly secured, to avoid trouble the next time the costume is put on.

Suitable fabrics are light-weight dress woollens, morocain or rayon, and for the women's more diaphanous costumes, various types of nylon can be used.

The ultimate in simplicity is a rectangle of material draped under the right arm and fastened on the left shoulder, surplus length being eliminated by pouching over the girdle. This is suitable for younger characters, slaves, etc.

Figures 21 and 22   Ionic chiton

The Ionic chiton consists of two rectangles of material fastened on each shoulder, or fastened at intervals along the top edges, thus forming rudimentary sleeves (*figure 22*). The back needs to be slightly narrower than the front to eliminate the tendency to slip, so that the neck opening is narrower at the back than at the front, which then forms a cowl neckline. Women have the edge over men here, since they can anchor to bra straps.

Figure 21   Ionic chiton

A good average measurement for making the Ionic chiton is double the width from elbow to elbow. The length will vary, depending upon what length tunic is required, but in each case a surplus should be allowed for take-up by a girdle, to give the authentic bloused effect. This type of tunic can also be worn full length, as it is for example in the famous statue of a charioteer at Delphi (*figure 21*). This chiton may be cut a little wider, and the folds and gathers pinned into position, then sewn on to a broad piece of tape from neck to elbow, and at the waist. The tape, which is sewn to the inside of the garment so that it does not show, prevents the folds slipping over the shoulders and down the upper arms.

If it is thought necessary in the interests of propriety to join

Figure 22   Ionic chiton, detail

up the sides, a more graceful effect is achieved by joining on the right side, about 4 to 6 in (10–15 cm) from the edge, thus leaving a loose flange which will conceal the seam in a fold.

Figure 23   Doric chiton

The Doric chiton is more elaborate, and takes slightly more material. The extra length is folded over, to fall from the shoulder. This over-fold may vary in length from just above waist length to hip length and is sometimes caught in at the waist by a girdle.

The Doric chiton was made from one long piece of material 12 in longer than the wearer's height and twice the distance from finger tip to finger tip, arms outstretched. Reduced to average measurements and present-day widths of material, this can be worked out as follows:

Man, 6 ft: 4 yards of 90 in sheeting, reduced to 84 in by 3 in hems top and bottom.

Woman, 5 ft 5 in: 4 yards 80 in sheeting, 2½ in top and bottom hems.

Cut the length into two and join side seams, leaving top 12 in free; finish these raw edges with a very narrow hem and fold over this extra 12 in. Stitch back and front together at shoulders.

Figure 23   Doric chiton

The women can anchor firmly to bra straps to prevent the garment sliding off the shoulders. For the men, make the back neck slightly narrower, about 10 in. The arms pass through the gaps left at the sides, and the surplus length is bloused over the girdle. The over-fold may have an ornamental border—the traditional Greek key pattern in gold is very effective on a white robe. Thick white cotton piping cord such as is used in upholstery is quite good enough for girdles. It is much cheaper than silk cord and does not come untied. Knot about 4 in from the end, and fray to form tassel.

Cloaks, stoles, veils etc., can be in a variety of lengths, sizes and textures. Apart from hemming raw edges, no making-up is necessary, and the whole effect will depend on careful draping and secure pinning. The length of tunic can vary according to the character, but the basic method is the same. Male slaves and peasants wear tunics of coarser material, in drab colours, sometimes slightly ragged, and merely caught together on the left shoulder.

Roman dress follows more or less the same lines, though slightly simpler and less voluminous. The women's equivalent to the Greek Ionic chiton, as already described, is the 'stola', worn with various similar draperies.

Men's tunics can either be like the Greek chiton, or cut in a simple magyar, seamed on the shoulders. With the full-length tunic is worn the toga, which is *not* just a long straight piece of material (though this will serve for lesser characters). At its full and correct size and shape, it is a semi-circle, about 6 yards by 7 ft. Nevil Truman, in *Historic Costuming*, gives very full and exact details of how it was arranged and worn. Even if these are not followed meticulously, a semi-circular toga is easier to arrange. It can be reduced in size if necessary.

Military accoutrements, both Greek and Roman, are rather beyond the scope of the average wardrobe mistress—although it is possible to contrive breastplates which look quite convincing on the stage—but the military tunic presents no difficulty. It can be considerably less voluminous than the civil one and is cut on magyar lines to the required length.

Figures 24 and 25   Greek warrior

The drawing shows a warrior taken from a vase painting of the 5th century BC. The cuirass can be made from buckram, steamed and moulded to the body, then painted, or of double hessian, sized and moulded, then painted. Lace together down each side with thonging or cord. Use the basic pattern, modified as in *figure 25*. This is worn over a short pleated tunic. To save material, make a pleated kilt on a waist band, and wear the breastplate over a sleeveless cotton T-shirt.

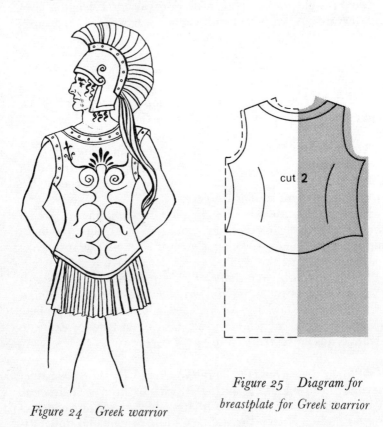

Figure 24　Greek warrior

Figure 25　Diagram for breastplate for Greek warrior

Figure 26　Roman soldier

The Roman soldier illustrated wears a cuirass which was made of metal strips. This is hardly practicable on the amateur stage, but overlapping flanges of plastic or polyurethane in dull grey would simulate steel. Make a linen, cotton or hessian 'body-belt' and machine a double strip to the lower edge, with the fold downwards. Let the next flanges overlap in turn; fold the edge of the top one to the inside and Copydex into place. Make broad shoulder straps in the same way. Between the cuirass and

Figure 26   Roman soldier

the tunic the soldier wears a leather jacket, which can also be made from polyurethane fabric. He can wear brown leggings, though these would not be worn in a play set in a hot climate. In Rome they were regarded as rather cissy but north of Hadrian's Wall they were probably not disparaged.

Instructions for making the buskin boot are given in the chapter on Accessories.

BYZANTINE

It seems odd that such a colourful period, sandwiched between Rome and the early Middle Ages, has not inspired any notable drama. Even Lucy Barton's comprehensive list does not include any specific plays, and merely suggests pageants and the like.

The period was about AD 500, and colourful mosaics in the church of San Vitale in Ravenna depict the Emperor Justinian and his wife Theodora—but nobody, it seems, put them in a play. However, since this book is a kind of miscellany, it seems pertinent to mention them, just in case *someone* wants to know.

James Laver's *Concise History of Costume* gives fascinating details of the appropriate costume, which was exciting and colourful. Although the cut of cloak and tunic was simple, the decoration is fantastic and shows a strong Oriental influence.

The tiara has the same outward slant as the Persian one previously mentioned, and the Empress wears a jewelled collar very much on Egyptian lines, but with the addition of an edging of pear-shaped gems.

A distinctive feature of the cloaks worn by some of her suite is a large contrasting rectangle, placed on the slant from just above the waist to above the knee. What the significance was I have been unable to find out, but it would serve to pinpoint the era if applied to a plain cloak of, say, the Norman period, similarly worn with the fastening on the right shoulder.

CHAPTER FOUR

RENAISSANCE

The costumes of this period were colourful and luxurious. Costly brocades, velvet, silks, satins, all contributed to the splendour, and however much the amateur wardrobe mistress has to scale down the extravagances, she can still, with some ingenuity, achieve the appearance, if not the reality, of the glamour and excitement. Although corresponding roughly to our own early Tudor period, there is a fluidity and elegance of line in contrast with the stiffness and constriction of Tudor costume.

As ever, the soft furnishing department is a happy hunting ground, particularly the remnant counter, since the richness of a piece of velvet or brocade can lift a costume out of the ordinary. Fur or fur fabric is almost a necessity, and even the tattiest bit of old coney gleams under the lights. A stencil and a paint spray can give the impression of stamped velvet; gum and glitter can work wonders, even with a piece of hessian. Braid, tassels, fringe, sequins, diamanté, all contribute to the overall effect.

The costumes which follow were adapted from contemporary paintings, and it is hoped that they will offer an interesting basis for a wide range of drama—Shakespeare's comedies and some of the tragedies, Marlowe, Tourneur, Kyd and others. They are not presented in any strict chronological order.

The beautifully fluted folds (and, in the case of *figure 33* the elegant fit) are achieved by cutting on the bias, and all these gowns should be allowed to hang for a day or two, so that they drop, after which the hem line can be straightened. This applies to the first six costumes, and *figure 31* gives the basic diagram for the first five. The widest material obtainable should be used; the centre fold is ironed out and each section is cut from single material. This probably entails crawling about on the floor, as no domestic table would be large enough to allow the material to be laid out flat. However, the final result is worth the discomfort.

29

In most cases some piecing will be needed, and the trimmed-off pieces must be joined on, as indicated in the diagram, on the straight edges. When joining two selvedges together, clip the tight edges of the seam allowance, otherwise they tend to show a pucker on the right side.

Choice of fabric is important. In most instances, a plain material is preferable, but if the designer really insists on a patterned fabric, an all-over design should be chosen, having no 'up-and-down'. Stripes and medallions are definitely unsuitable. In the originals, all the bias-cut materials are plain.

Hemlines tend to give trouble. After the finished garment has been hung, try it on the wearer and mark out the front hem, then, if time permits, hang again and if it still drops, adjust accordingly. One way of eliminating waste from later trimming away of 'drop' is to measure the true diagonal on the flat and mark with a pin or thread. Then hang a length up by its point, remeasure the diagonal, and compare the measurement obtained with the first one. The difference gives some guide for adjustment, and when cutting, allowance can be made by cutting an upward curve, at any rate on the front. If the back drops, it does not matter particularly but only adds to the train effect.

The costumes illustrated in the next four figures are all simple to make and rely for effect on richness of material and fur trimming. Although undeniably extravagant of material, as compensation each will provide ample scope for cannibalization in future productions. *Figures 27* and *28* are taken from the portrait of Count Arnolfini and his wife by van Eyck.

Figures 27, 28, 29, 30

Use the basic pattern adapted as in *figure 31* for the body of these gowns. Adaptations can be modified according to the budget. The lady's straight hanging sleeve in *figure 28* is trimmed with a deep ruche of 'self' material which should be made first and attached to the sleeve before sewing to the garment. Cut a straight strip about one-quarter the length of the main sleeve, and double its width. Mark out seven equidistant parallel lines and run double rows of gathering threads along these lines, using a strong spool thread and a loose top tension. Draw up to

Figure 27   Giovanni Arnolfini, after Jan van Eyck

fit sleeve, attach at lower edge first, turn right side out and attach top edge of ruche. If the fabric used is of fairly close weave, it is only necessary to top-stitch (preferably zig-zag), as the raw edge will not show from a distance. Machine along the gatherings to anchor to main sleeve. Close side seam to top of ruche; set into gown and trim slit with fur.

A plain undergown in a contrasting colour is worn with this costume. The train for the overgown should be as extravagant as expense permits but is not essential.

No special instructions are necessary for the making of the other three costumes as there is nothing complicated about the joining up of the sections. *Figure 27*, being sleeveless, needs another gown underneath. This is quite plain, with a high neck

Figure 28   Giovanni's wife

finished with a small band. The sleeves are set into plain cuffs.

Figure 29 has very wide set-in sleeves, the pattern for these is shown in *figure 31* and as wide a width of material as possible should be used. The sleeves fall to the hemline of the gown itself and lie in folds down each side.

Figure 30 shows the same very wide sleeves, fur trimmed as the main gown. The belt holds the folds of the gown in position, and the costume is worn with a high-necked undershirt.

All three men are depicted wearing hats. That in *figure 27* could be made in either fur fabric or velvet, following the general directions given in the chapter on headgear. Those in

Figure 29   Flowing knee-length tunic

Figure 30   Short fur-trimmed tunic

figures 29 and *30* can be made with felt brims and soft crowns. Brims can, if necessary, be cut off purchased hats (the remaining crown can be steamed into shape to serve as a page's 'fez'). Alternatively, do not cut off the brim but simply cut a large circular piece of material, gather round the edges, and sew over the original crown, covering the raw edges with a matching band. This leaves the hat available for future dismemberment and re-use.

Figure 32

This delightful costume presents no difficulties in cutting. Cut

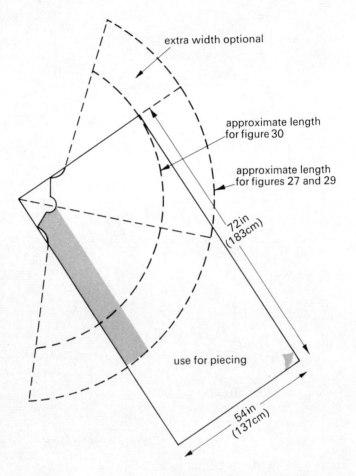

extra width optional

approximate length
for figure 30

approximate length
for figures 27 and 29

72in
(183cm)

use for piecing

54in
(137cm)

Figure 31 (a)   Diagram for bias-cut gowns and tunics

as shown in *figure 31* and make the puffed sleeve as described in *figure 48*, using contrasting material. Trim the bodice with rosettes of ribbon or braid, and finish the round neck with a narrow band of fur.

The turban headdress is made on a close-fitting skull-cap foundation cut from an old felt hat in a suitable colour. Cut a bias strip to fit round the head without stretching, having a width of up to 27 in (70 cm) depending upon the degree of exaggeration required. Line with thin foam rubber or Vilene;

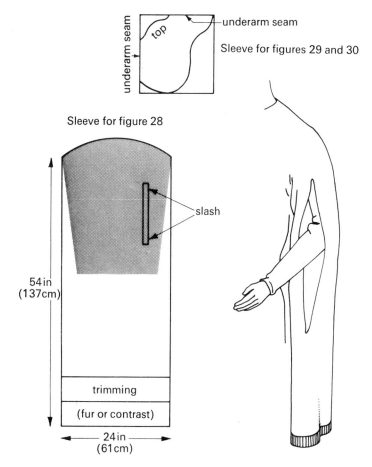

Figure 31 (b) Diagram for sleeves for figures 28, 29 and 30

baste at long edges and join short edges. Oversew long edges
together and flatten this seam. Attach the resultant 'dough-
nut' to the skull-cap. Make nine contrasting strips of graduated
lengths—one short one for centre back, to conceal back seam,
and draw in the roll firmly. Vary the others according to the
finished size required—anything from about 15 in (38 cm) to
25 in (64 cm) for the fantastic. Space these strips round the cap
and stitch on the underside. Lap each strip over the roll,
tightening it slightly, and stitch to the crown about 3 in (8 cm)

Figure 32   Detail from a mural in Padua—'April'

from the lower edge, so that the roll is held in place and does
not flop down over the forehead.

Figures 33 and 34

This is a Venetian gown, severe and bias cut. Its plain elegance
makes it suitable for a wide range of characters. The style has
such simplicity that it is almost timeless. It could fit into some
of the early Plantagenet histories, and might also solve the
problem of style in some of the plays of a legendary or indeter-
minate date. Lady Macbeth might wear it; so might Imogen in
Cymbeline, or Hermione in *Winter's Tale*.

It needs careful cutting and fitting, and the pattern must first

Figure 33   Plain bias-cut gown

be checked with the wearer's measurements, particularly the neck-to-waist measurement. A 22-in zip in the centre back ensures a closer fit. Use the basic sheath-line pattern and the plain sleeve (*figure 34*), and cut the sleeve also on the bias for a tighter fit, making an opening at the wrist. As with all these wide-necked gowns, the back must not be cut too low. Machine tape 'stays' at neck edges and across tops of sleeves. The tape or elastic method will help keep it in place. Trim neck and wrist with a narrow band of black ribbon velvet.

This is one of the instances where the front should be measured and adjusted by the hanging method previously mentioned, before cutting out, so that the front hem will take an upward curve.

The style may be varied by slitting the side seam up to the

thigh, midway between waist and knee, and either wearing the gown over a contrasting kirtle, or inserting a contrasting 'fishtail' in the side seam. Provided the wearer's figure is sufficiently trim and slender, this gown worn over bra and tights can be superbly effective.

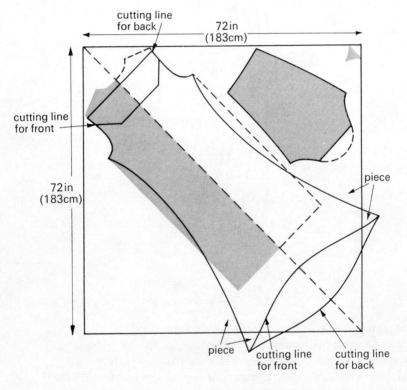

Figure 34   Diagram for Fig. 33

Figures 35 and 36

Although this was primarily a military costume (*c* 1530) as worn by German mercenaries, or Landsknecht, the idea of slashing seems to have had a wide impact on male costume of the time, and can be used generally with great effect.

The slashings are actual, not applied, so must be mounted on a non-woven interlining, preferably using a swing-needle

Figure 35   German Landsknecht: slashed doublet and hose

machine; in addition, doublet and breeches need to be lined. White shirting or Terylene is suitable.

Cut the doublet from the basic pattern, modified as in *figure 36* with a centre back opening, and leave the back un-slashed. Cut an interlining for the front in Vilene or similar non-woven material, and baste the two pieces together at all edges. Place this section with right side down, and draw a diagonal line on the Vilene from about 4 in (10 cm) below left shoulder to about 4 in (10 cm) from point of waist/side seam. Draw two parallel lines each side of this line, spaced equidistant between waist and right shoulder (see diagram). Baste along these lines. If a swing-needle machine is available, set the stitch length to 'Fine' and stitch width to about 3 cm

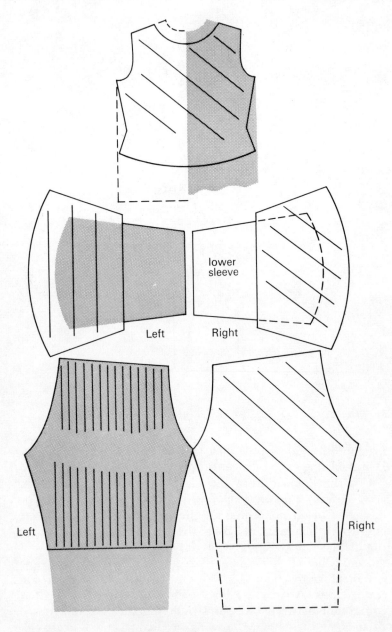

Figure 36   Diagram for Fig. 35

(Singer No. 3). Work two lines of zig-zag stitching on either side of the marked line, about ⅛ in (3 cm) apart. Work five bartack stitches on the turn, and finish off similarly. (NB. Many of the more sophisticated machines now have a buttonhole selector which takes care of this operation, including the double-width bartacks at each end of the slash.) Repeat for each marked line, and leave the actual slashing until the garment is completed.

The inner lining—necessary to give the appearance of a shirt—needs to be fairly voluminous, so that it can be pulled through the slashings. Cut from the white material, slightly wider and longer than the front doublet, and gather in the surplus on the seams. Mount the whole section on a close-fitting lining. Line the back similarly, and machine all four layers in one operation (counting Vilene as one layer). This will give the finished garment a solidity in keeping with the rather rumbustious character who would probably wear it (Henry VIII, for instance).

The sleeve is evolved from the puffed sleeve which seems to appear time and again down the years. Modify the basic sleeve as in *figure 36* and repeat the foregoing operations. The right sleeve is slashed diagonally, the left, laterally. The upper 'shirt' sleeve section is enlarged, and the whole sleeve is mounted on a close-fitting inner lining. Baste together the outer and inner sleeve. Baste lower sleeve to inner lining and pleat lower edge of upper sleeve to match upper edge on fore-arm section. Machine both sections firmly to lining. Pleat top of puff to sleeve head and machine together. (It makes for easier handling if all these various layers are sewn together before being matched to the next section.)

Join shoulder seams; set sleeves into armhole; machine side and underarm seams in one continuous operation. (Note: When setting sleeve to armhole, have the body section on top, so that the machine foot rides more easily over the pleated upper sleeve.)

Fill in neckline with a 'gilet' in the same material as the shirt, and add a shirt frill at wrist.

The breeches are made in the same way, modifying the pyjama trouser pattern as indicated in diagram, and marking out the slashes; the right leg is slashed diagonally and the left one perpendicularly—almost to ribbons. Mount on under breeches, cut close fitting on 'canion' lines, omitting the 'shirt' layer. Set on a band fastening below knee, and tie with sash garters.

It will probably be more convenient to join breeches and doublet at the waist, making a 'combination' type of garment; this is considerably less hazardous than 'separates'.

The final operation is the careful cutting of the slashes. Using sharp pointed scissors, slit carefully between all the lines of stitching. Pull the 'shirt' through into puffs, and tack at intervals to keep in place. Tack the slashes together as shown in sketch, and sew a small contrasting bow at each point.

The hat has a stiffened brim to which a soft crown is attached, rather like a Tudor bonnet. Finish off with feathers.

Figures 37 and 38

These costumes are taken from a painting by Carpaccio of two courtesans. The well-known original shows two supremely bored looking women, sumptuously dressed—just waiting.

The basic line is almost Regency, consisting of a tiny bodice and a high-waisted skirt falling straight to the floor. Modify the basic bodice pattern by trimming away from shoulder to arm-pit, as shown in *figure 38*, but be careful not to cut the back of the bodice too low, otherwise it will fall off the shoulders. Use the tape or elastic method to keep in place.

Use the plain sleeve, slashed from shoulder to wrist, and cut a wider undersleeve from lawn or nylon. Make a narrow hem on the cut edges, and position the upper sleeve over the under-sleeve. Pin securely at underarm edges, then seam all outer edges together in one operation, leaving the free upper sleeve to be tied across with cord or ribbon. Do this tying on the wearer, to get a close fit. Then pull the undersleeve through the gaps, to give the correct puffed appearance. Join sleeve to bodice at underarm, and bridge the gap between back and front bodice with a narrow band of material in the same way as in the costume described in chapter 5, *figure 59*.

In the original painting both costumes are made in two contrasting fabrics. The one on the right is in gold satin, with a dark velvet bodice and matching band at the hem. The band at

(a)

(b)

Figure 37   Two courtesans, after Carpaccio

the neck is trimmed with drop beads. The one on the left has a
deep red skirt, the bodice and sleeves being in a darker colour
covered with gold embroidery. Neither of these gowns takes an
inordinate amount of material, so a relatively expensive fabric
could be used.

Figures 39 and 40

This costume is taken from a portrait by Cranach. The elabor-
ately fluted skirt which is the chief attraction of this gown is
achieved more economically than would at first appear, since
the flutes conceal seams. Either 36 in, 39 in, 45 in or 54 in

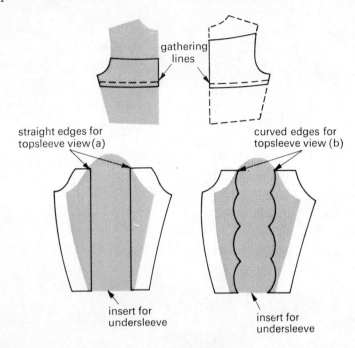

gathering lines

straight edges for
topsleeve view (a)

curved edges for
topsleeve view (b)

insert for
undersleeve

insert for
undersleeve

Figure 38   Diagram for Fig. 37

(91 cm, 1 m, 115 cm or 137 cm) material can be used. The most
convenient and economical is 45 in (115 cm)—full length skirt,
average height. 3¼ yd (or 3 m allowing slightly more) gives a
finished hemline of about 4½ yd (3·75 m). Mark out lines on the
fabric as indicated in *figure 40*. This makes 19 gores each 9 in
(23 cm) at the hem and 3 in (7·5 cm) at the waist. The two
end pieces forming half a gore are joined at the straight edge to
form the centre back seam. (The finished measurement will be
reduced by the seam allowances, so that the waist measurement
will need only slight adjustment by means of pleating.)

Non-woven interlining is necessary to keep the flutes rounded
out, but this need not be taken up to the waist, as it would make
too much bulk. Cut from the width of 36 in (1 m) Vilene and
pin to gores from hemline upwards, thus leaving unstiffened the
top 9 in (or 15 cm if using 1 m width).

Before joining the gores together, appliqué the three ornamental bands of contrasting material. Position these with care

Figure 39   *Portrait of a princess, after Cranach*

(as shown in the drawing) as they must match up to form continuous bands. They need not be cut on the bias as the flare is slight, and if the lower edge is attached first, a couple of pinch pleats will make the top edge lie flat. Top-stitch using zig-zag, or run a double row of straight stitching if a swing-needle is not available. If the material frays badly, a small single hem will have to be turned under before stitching.

Using the basic flared pattern, cut an underskirt with a finished hemline of about $2\frac{1}{2}$ yd (220 cm), having a centre back seam. Mark out lines as indicated in *figure 40*—ten on the front section and four on each back section.

It is easier to make up the skirt in sections: front, left back, right back. Join together eleven gores for the front, and four and

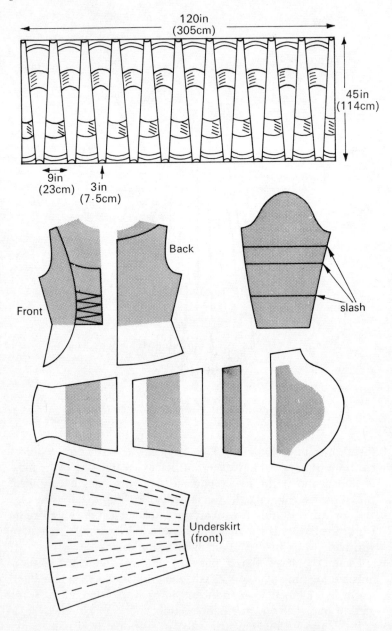

Figure 40   Diagram for Fig. 39

a half each for left and right back. Lay the front of the main skirt flat, with seams uppermost. Baste together one main and underskirt side seam (have this seam farthest away from you, with bulk of main skirt towards you so that this can be pushed away as each seam is dealt with). Fold back underskirt along the marked line, and attach at this line to first seam of main skirt, using fairly strong cotton, and about 1 in (2 cm) tacks. Repeat this operation with each marked line, ending with side seams. Treat back sections similarly, but join centre back seams separately—first the main skirt, then lining, in each case leaving open about 9 in (23 cm) for zipper. Baste together the edges of back opening and insert zipper. Join side seams of skirt and finish off with a waistband.

The bodice consists of a little jacket with wide front lacing over a chemise, and here again it makes for easier dressing if it is made with a centre back opening.

Use a panelled pattern, modified as in *figure 40* and make the chemise in a contrasting material to match the sleeves. The lacing can be faked.

The sleeves are in five sections, puffed and banded. Slash basic plain sleeve at the points indicated in diagram and enlarge as indicated by black lines. Gather top and middle sections (*figure 39*), and attach narrow contrasting bands of the same material as the skirt bands. The cuff is also made of the contrasting fabric. Mount sleeve on a plain lining. Mark lines where original pattern was slashed, and anchor puffs at these points.

Trim edge of bodice with contrast, and insert zipper at centre back. As this neckline is so wide, tapes or an elastic can be passed under the arms and tied centre back, to prevent slipping.

Several petticoats are necessary, to give body to the skirt, but these should be stock items in the wardrobe. Starched cotton sheeting gives solidity, and additional stiffness can be gained from a broad hem padded with newspaper.

Figures 41 and 42

Another elegantly simple gown suitable for a wide range of characters. It is adapted from Carnevale's *Birth of the Virgin*. The original is colourful and attractive: the sleeves are olive

Figure 41   Gown with overgown and contrasting sleeves

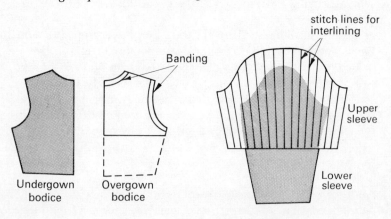

Figure 42   Diagram for Fig. 41

green velvet, the kirtle a delicate strawberry-pink with a mid-
night-blue band at the waist; the overgown is white or cream.
This could be made separately, affording the possibilities of
some variation of costume for the character during the course of
the play.

The bodice of the kirtle is completely plain. The skirt is fairly
full, attached to the bodice with organ pleats, and the contrasting belt is worn high under the bust, not at the waist. (The little
knot of cord seen through the slit of the overgown may have
closed a placket giving access to a pocket.)

The overgown is high waisted, the bodice ending just under
the bust, and is cut from the basic pattern, modified as in
figure 42. The plain full skirt, as voluminous as material permits,
should not be so long as to be unmanageable, though the
fashion of the day was to carry it bunched up in the front. For
stage wear this would be hampering, so it is better to make
it only floor length. When carried it will reveal the undergown.
This skirt has a deep slit down the side from the bodice, and the
side seam is joined only from below the knee to the ground. As
with the undergown, the skirt is joined to the bodice with organ
pleats. The easiest way to achieve these is to head the inside of
the skirt with deep curtain tape. The cords are then drawn up
to fit back and front of bodice, leaving the underarm open.

For ease of dressing, the overgown can be slipped over the
head and fastened each side under the arms.

The sleeve is yet another variant of the two-piece puffed
sleeve. The lower sleeve is close fitting to just above the elbow;
the upper sleeve is also set in organ pleats at lower sleeve and
armhole. It is mounted on an interlining, and the pleats sewn
into place before joining to lower sleeve and armhole. Mark the
interlining with straight lines as indicated in diagram and
baste it to upper sleeve along each line. Fold on the wrong
side along each marked line, and machine about $\frac{1}{4}$ in (0·5 cm)
from folds, taking care that the main material is caught into the
seam. Repeat for each marked line.

Finish neckline and armhole of overgown with a narrow band
of 'self' colour in a contrasting texture. The overgown would
look well in a soft woollen material with a matt surface. The
undergown, in the original, might well have been velvet.

The skirt should not be skimped, but as it is not bias cut

or flared, it will provide a straight length of material for re-use, so one can afford to be generous. Extra fullness can be given to the back by using the 'standard' skirt method (*figure 43*).

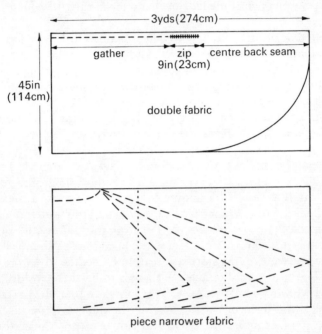

Figure 43 '*Standard*' *skirt*

Figures 44 and 45

The half-length drawing is taken from a mural by Veronese; the full-length figure is adapted from a portrait by Bronzino. Each has a low-cut bodice cut straight across the top, and to a point at the waist, though this is not as exaggerated as the later style.

Use the bodice section of the basic pattern and adapt as shown in *figure 45*. Slash straight across the front, just above the armpit, as indicated. Make the lower section in the main fabric and cut the yoke in double net. The back yoke may be made in net or in self fabric.

To decorate the yoke, first cut a template in white paper—either pattern paper, tissue paper or even kitchen paper. On

(a)

(b)

Figure 44   Gown with lattice yoke

this template mark out with a felt pen the lattice design. This will show through the net as a guide.

There is considerable scope for decoration. In the Bronzino portrait, it is in narrow gold braid, with a pearl at each intersection, whereas the Veronese shows the lattice pattern in white (which could be carried out in narrow white ribbon), with a topaz-coloured jewel at each crossing. Colour is entirely a matter for the designer.

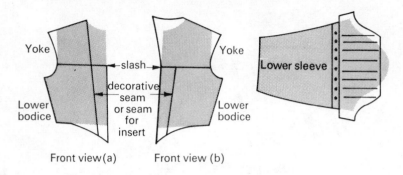

Figure 45   Diagram for Fig. 44

Pin or baste the braid or ribbon, taking in the paper as well. Machine into place, then tear away the paper afterwards. This keeps the crossways lines from warping.

The sleeve method has already been described. The front 'stomacher' can be laid on and stitched to the main bodice.

Use the 'standard' skirt over a small hip roll.

Figures 46 and 47

Many of the sleeves in this period were not seamed to the garments, but were tied in with points—cord or ribbon lacings terminating in aglets (a corruption of *aiguillettes*), the making of which is described in the chapter on accessories. Sleeves were therefore quite an important accessory in themselves, to the extent of being specified separately in costume descriptions. In a Privy Council report concerning Katherine Howard after her arrest, it is mentioned that 'to the queen's grace ye must appoint six French Hoods . . . likewise, as many pairs of sleeves, six gowns . . .' (Strickland).

Tied sleeves can form a useful method of making variations in a costume.

The top sleeve is very simple. Use the long 'Bishop' sleeve basic pattern, enlarged as in *figure 47*. (If this sleeve is cut in one piece and the decoration sewn on by hand and not machined, the latter can be removed when necessary and the sleeve used again.) Lawn, Terylene or nylon are suitable fabrics, in white, preferably, as this represents the chemise. Cut a plain inner

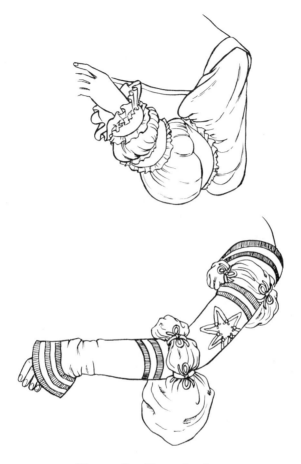

Figure 46   Alternative sleeves

sleeve of flesh-coloured net. Close underarm seams of both inner and outer sleeve. Mount the white sleeve on lining, basting at wrist, forearm and just above the elbow. Cut three plain strips of the main fabric and trim both edges with a contrasting ribbon frill. Machine the short edges to form 'bracelets' and stitch these to the main sleeve by hand.

The full white sleeve, with the 'bracelets' and lining removed, can later become a component part of the second sleeve shown at *figure 46* and this in turn can be made in detachable sections. Cut it from the basic pattern, slashed where indicated on diagram and extended at the wrist to form the 'goblet' shape, similar to the Cranach portrait described earlier. Any amount of trimming may be lavished on this sleeve, which could itself be made from a remnant of brocade, satin or velvet, so adding a touch of luxury to an otherwise plain gown.

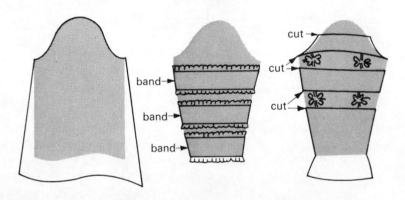

Figure 47 Diagrams for Fig. 46

The upper section and the cuff should be stiffened with Vilene, and the cuff should be lined with a contrasting material.

Make the ties of cord or ribbon, and space four sets round each section, as shown in the sketch. (Only two are shown, but of course, there must be ties on the under side as well.) Pull the undersleeve through the gaps. It will save time in dressing if the sections are fitted first, and tacked into position firmly enough to hold them but not so firmly that they cannot later be separated.

Figure 48 Puffed sleeve

The puffed sleeve is one of the most versatile sleeves ever designed. It reappears at intervals from Plantagenet times down to the present day. I have used it in productions as different as *Hamlet* and *The Cherry Orchard*, and it reappeared in the pattern books in the late 1960s.

It consists of two pieces—a close-fitting lower sleeve and a puffed upper section, and the proportions of these two sections can vary considerably, according to period. The whole sleeve is

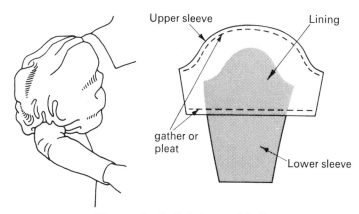

Figure 48   Puffed sleeve, with diagram

mounted on and attached to a lining, to keep the puffed section in place.

Slash the basic sleeve across, either above or below the elbow. Cut the lower sleeve plain and close fitting; cut the upper sleeve wider and deeper, depending upon the degree of exaggeration required. Interline with Vilene or similar. Baste interlining to sleeve, and apply any necessary decoration at this stage.

Place lining flat on table, and baste lower sleeve, right side uppermost. Reduce the lower edge of the upper sleeve to the same measurement as the top of the lower sleeve, either by small pinch pleats or by gathering, depending upon the thickness of the material. With right sides together, match the gathered edge to top of lower sleeve, baste, machine both sections to lining. Gather or pleat the curved top edge to armhole edge of lining, and set into garment before finishing side seams. The surplus of the puff on the underarm seam can be pleated in at the elbow when machining the side seam.

As an alternative, the puff can be replaced by paned strips, rather like the Virago sleeve mentioned in the chapter on English variations.

Figures 49 and 50   Doge's cap

The doge was the chief magistrate in the Venetian and Genoese republics. So far as Shakespeare was concerned, he was the Duke of Venice, and appears both in the *Merchant of Venice*

Figure 49   Doge's cap

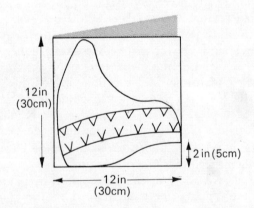

12in
(30cm)

2 in (5cm)

12in
(30cm)

Figure 50   Diagram for doge's cap

and in *Othello*. It therefore seems pertinent to offer some guidance in the making of his distinctive headdress.

Probably felt is the most suitable material, though any close-woven thick matt fabric could be used.

Cut two sections from the pattern shown at *figure 50*. The centre front seam should be tightened by feeding under the machine foot rather than pulling away from it. This will eliminate any tendency to show a ridge. The cap must fit tightly, and any necessary adjustment can be made on the back seam.

Trim with a band of embroidery or brocade, as shown in the drawing.

As this would be a permanent item in the wardrobe, it is worth taking a little more trouble in the making, and it should be lined. If the material selected is not stiff enough to hold its shape, cut an interlining of non-woven material such as Vilene. Anchor this to the cap sections with dabs of Copydex, placed well clear of the sewing line to avoid clogging the needle. This is not a difficult cap to make and is most useful in any production with a Venetian setting.

CHAPTER FIVE

VARIATIONS

This chapter is intended to offer variations on the basic English costumes featured in my earlier book,* which could only deal with the general 'line' of a period. Changes in costume are never drastic and sudden; they creep in here and there, modifying a line, trying out a new length, moving the waistline, dropping the shoulder line; they are never static, but always interesting. They appear, they disappear, and then they bob up again, and even in one's own lifetime, one often gets the feeling, 'this is where I came in'.

On a more practical plane, these variations help the wardrobe mistress to maintain a freshness of approach and to combat staleness. At all costs one must never sink into the mental attitude that congeals into a sentimental 'dear old so-and-so wore that in . . .' whatever it was being staged a decade ago.

None of the following is a complete costume in itself, but each is capable of being teamed with another costume and giving it a new look, to stimulate the interest of the audience, and to stretch an exiguous budget by re-using material from an earlier production.

When I first started 'costuming' I found this cannibalization rather shattering, having put hours of meticulous work into a gown only worn for one production. But I soon learned not to put in such detailed work, and became quite ruthless, rather to the dismay of some of the 'old guard', who always enquired 'what happened to . . .?' My most appreciated compliment came from the drama critic on the local paper, who said 'thank goodness *that's* gone—it could have played the part with no-one inside!'

Figure 51   Elizabethan overgown

Anyone who has spent any time in an Elizabethan cottage will

---

* *Stage Costumes and How to Make Them*, Pitman 1969.

have been shiveringly aware of some good old Elizabethan draughts. It is not surprising that the girls of the day evolved their own version of the maxi-coat. The 'loose-bodied gown' presented by the ill-used tailor for Petruchio's approval is an example. Such an overgown is a useful piece of wardrobe, as it can vary a costume, indicate a change of scene or the passage of time; it was the virtual equivalent of our indispensable cardigan, and is depicted in portraits up till about 1625. If the budget allows, make it in velvet, which can be spray-dyed for added richness.

Use pieces C and D of the basic pattern (female) modified as in *figure 51*. Cut lining to the same pattern (with front edges to selvedge, if possible) but 4 in (10 cm) shorter at the bottom. As this is an edge-to-edge garment worn fastened from neck to hem it is not really necessary to cut a front facing, but an interfacing some 4 in (10 cm) wide adds body. Baste this to front edges before joining seams.

Assemble in the following sequence: join side seams (but *not* shoulder seams) of gown and of lining. Place right sides together and machine: front neck, back neck, armholes and lower edge. Snip curved edges of neck and armholes and turn to right side by pulling through at front edge. Flatten lining seams with thumb-nail. Now place back and front shoulder seams of gown (not of lining) together, and machine. Flatten seam, fold in turning allowance of back lining, push raw edge of front lining underneath and slip-stitch into place.

This leaves the front lining loose, and before slip-stitching this into place, turn it back as far as the side seams and anchor side seams of lining to side seams of gown with long basting stitches.

Mark out on front edges for points (see 'Accessories'), seven, eight or nine in number. Use cord or ribbon and allow 18 in to 20 in (50 cm) for each knot. The portraits of the time show two kinds of knot: a simple bow, in which case each tie should be about the same length—9 in to 10 in (25 cm); or, alternatively, the bow sometimes had only one loop, so that the proportionate lengths each side would be about one-third to two-thirds. Sew these firmly into place exactly on the seam allowance ($\frac{5}{8}$ in (1·5 cm). Turn in seam allowance, baste to interlining, and slip-stitch lining into place.

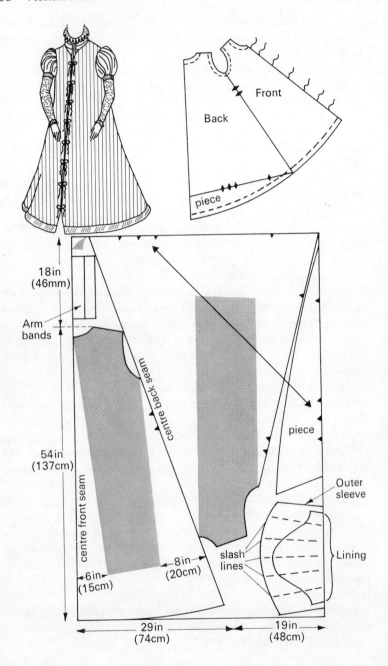

This is the basic gown. Trimmings are a matter of taste and availability and can be added down the front and round the hem line. Fur, galon, gold braid, gold-sprayed lace, etc., and any such elaboration need only be stuck on with Copydex.

A short sleeve, puffed and paned, can be attached to the main gown by means of points. Use the basic pattern at the 'short sleeve' line, which is indicated on most bought patterns, slightly enlarged as indicated in diagram. Cut a pair of sleeves in the main gown fabric, and divide (from shoulder to hem) into five sections and insert contrasting strips of roughly equal width as the main colour. Pleat in surplus at top and bottom, and mount on lining cut to the 'actual' sleeve. Finish bottom of sleeve with a straight band in main colour.

These gowns were sometimes finished with a small, close-fitting standing collar topped with the small ruff of the under-gown.

The two portraits from which these descriptions are taken can both be found in Cunnington's *Picture History of English Costume*. The first (No. 71) is an engraving of Queen Elizabeth I and is dated 1559. The second (No. 114) is a portrait of Lady Dorothy Carey, dated 1615–20. The overgown in this instance is not fastened in front. It has long hanging sleeves open from the armhole, and the fronts and hemline are lavishly orna-mented with gold embroidery.

Both styles should be cut as voluminously as possible. If a closed gown to be worn over a farthingale is required, the lower hem must, of course, be slightly more than the lower hem of the undergown. The proportions given are not arbitrary, but are based on an average bust measurement of 34 in–36 in (87–92 cm); they could, if necessary, be cut down by diminishing the outward swing of the side seams and centre back seams, and 'closing up' the pattern accordingly. The lower hem measure-ment indicated by the diagrams is about $4\frac{1}{2}$ yd (4 m approx.).

Figure 52   '*Dutch' waist with wheel farthingale*

Anne of Denmark, queen of James I, apparently had 'made over' many of the gowns in Elizabeth I's extensive wardrobe.

Figure 51 (opposite)   *Elizabethan overgown, with diagram*

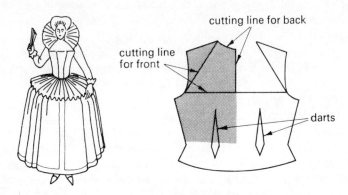

Figure 52 'Dutch' waist with wheel farthingale

Possibly this is why she continued to wear the rather out-moded cartwheel farthingale which persisted, though reduced in size, until after her death in 1619. A contemporary portrait by Geerharts shows a 'frounced' skirt, the bodice having, instead of the usual point, a rounded 'Dutch waist' which is not only more comfortable in wear, but easier to make. Cut the bodice to fit snugly to just below the natural waistline, and make the skirt from a straight piece of material about $3\frac{1}{2}$–4 yd (3–$3\frac{1}{2}$ m) long. If plain reversible material is used, 54 in (138 cm) in width, this needs no shaping at all, and leaves a nice chunk of material for future use. Simply measure the required length from waist to ground, allowing for take-up by the farthingale, and machine both edges of a piece of Rufflette tape along this line. Join seam of skirt, and draw up strings of the tape so that the skirt fits tightly at the waist. The frill falls outwards, concealing the tape. This skirt does not trail and, depending upon the height of the wearer, can be instep length, with a frounce of some 9 in (23 cm). If the wearer be more diminutive, the excess can be added to the lower hem, rather than cut away and wasted.

If using patterned material with a right and wrong side, the frounce will have to be cut separately, joined at the waist with the seam on the right side and the Rufflette tape machined over the raw edges.

The sleeves of this period were fairly plainly cut, the or-

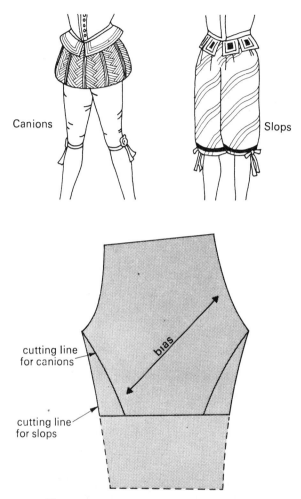

Canions

Slops

cutting line
for canions

bias

cutting line
for slops

Figure 53   Canions and slops, with diagram

namentation being confined to epaulettes, braiding etc.,
finished with a turn-back, lace-edged, cuff.

Figure 53   Canions and 'slops'

Canions seem to have been the Tudor equivalent of 'long
johns', and could, if necessary, be contrived out of cotton tights

painted or tie-dyed. They were worn under the puffed trunk hose, and were close fitting to the knee, with the stockings rolled over the ends. One presumes the latter were kept up by garters, but in practice it would seem less hazardous to attach them firmly to the canions.

The portraits of the time show canions of brocade, and of a contrasting colour to the trunk hose and doublet. They need careful cutting, and must fit well. Use Piece E of the basic (pyjama) pattern, modified as shown. A better fit can be obtained by cutting on the bias, if the design of the material permits. Make up according to pattern instructions for pants or shorts, but baste and fit before finally sewing.

Slop-hose, or just 'slops' can be cut on the same lines, but slightly fuller and longer, and loose at the knee, so that the stockings can go underneath. A portrait of James I of England dated 1605 shows him wearing such hose, which are of plain material (possibly satin) trimmed with a broad stripe of braid down the sides and round the bottom. The loops of the sash garters hang down below the edges of the hose.

Use the same pattern, modified as shown—it is not necessary to cut on the bias.

Figure 54 Gown with dropped shoulder line: Stuart Restoration

This décolleté bodice appears in a portrait dated 1649, just before Commonwealth austerity clamped down. After the Restoration the demure lace neckerchieves were tossed away, the neckline slid right off the shoulders, and the style reappears in a portrait dated between 1660 and 1670.

The cutting requires some care. The back neck must not be cut too low, the bodice must fit tightly, and it must be lined. In addition, the front should be interlined with Vilene or other non-woven interlining.

The shoulder line is moved to the front by extending the bodice back over the shoulder and dropping the seam almost to the armpit. The actual seam is left open to reveal the white under bodice. The ballooned sleeve, slashed and left unbuttoned to reveal the white lawn undersleeve, extends just over the elbow. The front bodice is buttoned over the white under-bodice, which also appears as a plain, narrow edging at the

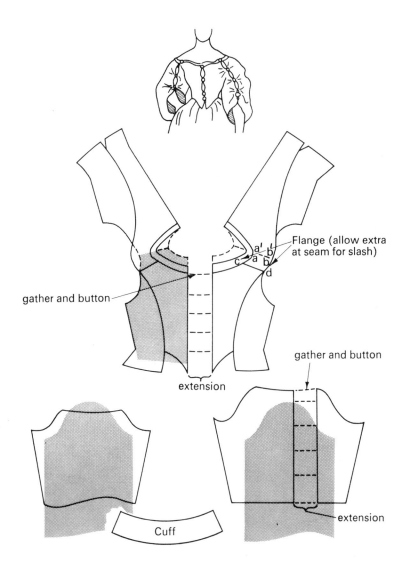

Flange (allow extra at seam for slash)

gather and button

gather and button

extension

extension

Cuff

Figure 54 Gown with dropped shoulder line: Stuart Restoration

neckline. The most economical way of achieving this effect is to make the bodice lining of material suitable for the under-bodice. White Terylene lawn is a good choice.

Instead of using the basic pattern, select a pattern which is styled on princess lines, having a panelled front with a seam running into the armhole seam. Trace on to a sheet of paper (pattern paper, thin brown paper or even newspaper) the centre front and centre back panels, down to a point about 6 in below the natural waistline. With a contrasting colour, mark the modifications indicated by black lines. Cut *front* panel first, trim away on line c–d, and move this section so that the line a–b marries with the line a^i–b^i of back panel. Trace and cut. The side front and side back panels will not need amendment, but the sleeve will need modification as indicated in the diagram.

Cut front panels, side front panels, side back panels and back panels to pattern as modified. The bodice is open at centre front and centre back so there is no need to aim for folds. Also, using centre front panel, cut interlining, and trim away seam allowance at shoulder, neck, front and lower edges. Cut bodice lining, placing centre front of pattern about $2\frac{1}{2}$ in (7 cm) from fold. At neck edge and shoulder seam, cut a $2\frac{1}{2}$ in (7 cm) extension, and before removing pattern, mark with tracing paper or tailor tacks the seam lines at shoulder, neck and front edges. (These extensions form the simulated undergown.) Cut side front, side back and centre back panels the same as main garment, except that the back neckline must have a similar extension to that allowed on the front.

Place centre front panels right side down, and superimpose interlining, pin together the raw edges at armhole and side fronts; fold over seam allowance at neck, front and lower edges, and baste.

Open out front panel of underbodice and spread flat on table. Fold neck extension outwards by about half its width. Match together the raw edges at armhole and side fronts, of under and outer bodice, and pin or baste together. Lap the neck edge of outer bodice over raw edge of the folded down extension and baste; match centre front of outer bodice to marked line on under bodice, and baste. Top-stitch by machine along shoulder line, neck edge and down front. (Repeat for other side of bodice.) This leaves a wide stripe of lawn at the centre front. Bring the two top points of the bodice together in a box pleat, and stitch together for about 1 in (2·5 cm). Repeat this operation at lower edge, to form a point, and stitch together for about 3 in (8 cm). Divide the remainder of the 'stripe' into equal sections (about three), run gathering threads across, draw up, and stitch the two sections of the main bodice together, trimming each point with a fancy button or knot of braid.

Repeat for back neck (omitting interlining). Lap shoulder seam of back bodice over front extension of under bodice and top-stitch. Bring the two points together, sew firmly, and trim to match front.

Match lining to main sections of side front and side back panels, pin or baste together, and join to front and back bodice respectively, as far as the waist only. Join side seams to waist only. Fold back and neaten the lappets so formed, and also the centre front point. In wear, the skirt band passes under the front point and over the rest of the lappets.

The sleeves of this style of gown can remain as the rather stiff, formal type, pleated both into the armhole and into a wide stiffened cuff. Cut sleeve and cuff as at *figure 54*, using the same tracing method as suggested for the bodice.

Alternatively, cut the outer sleeve as above, and cut an undersleeve in lawn (as used for bodice lining). The outer sleeve seam, which meets the bodice at the open shoulder seam, is left open, or can be buttoned, similarly to bodice front. Neaten seam edges and lower edge; join seam of undersleeve, and pin or baste together at armhole. Arrange fullness in pleats or gathers and set into armhole. This is one of the sleeves which cannot be inserted flat before joining the side seams. It is a casual sleeve of the sort favoured by Nell Gwynn, and can either hang loosely over the forearm, or have the lower edge of the undersleeve gathered into a deep frill, according to taste.

Colour is always a matter of taste, but the style does seem to suggest reseda green, dull gold, turquoise blue, muted pink, or black, in gleaming satin, and certainly not a patterned material.

The dropped shoulder may be found rather to impede movement, and the style should not be chosen for a role portraying a boisterous type of wench.

Figure 55   Regency ball-gown (c. *1811*)

Figures 55 and 56   Regency ball-gown (*c 1811*)

This is an elegant gown with a contrasting under-petticoat and sleeve slashings, which can, in fact, be made as part of the same garment. The bodice is very décolleté, and is best attached firmly to a wired bra with wide-set straps.

As with the Regency gown which is discussed next, the back and front bodice are cut in one piece, using the basic bodice pattern modified as in *figure 56*.

Make a newspaper template of the basic sleeve pattern, and slash from armhole to wrist as indicated on diagram, taking the matching notch as a starting point. Transpose the pieces so that the original underarm seam is eliminated. A straight piece

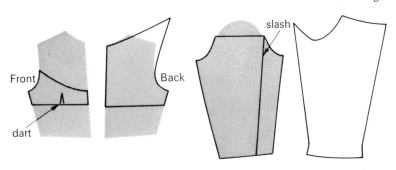

Figure 56   Diagram for Fig. 55

of material about 4 in (10 cm) wide is inserted, and the resulting seams trimmed with braid or galon, and the slit is caught together at four equidistant points. The same trimming out- lines the armhole (armscye), the sleeve edges, the front panel, the hem line, and the triangular insets. The back of the skirt is plain, with only very slight fullness; the front has a contrasting, slightly flared inset, on to which are appliquéd the triangular pieces indicated.

A small inset matching the underskirt can fill in the décolleté if necessary.

Figures 57 and 58   Regency gown (c 1812)

This gown, from a portrait by Lawrence, is dainty, effective, and simple to cut. It has a high-waisted bodice, cut from the basic pattern as in *figure 58*. The shoulder seam is eliminated, and the bodice back extended nearly to the armpit. The lower front bodice is virtually a bra-shaped section. To keep this bodice from slipping in wear, attach tape or elastic at the point where the two sections of the bodice meet, and tie at the back. The puffed sleeve is mounted on a plain lining, and if the fabric used is very soft, the bouffant effect is achieved with iron- on Vilene. The skirt is plain and straight in front, with a little extra fullness at the back—gathered, if the material is very fine, or slightly flared. The lower hem is finished with a full flounce.

A wide contrasting sash, and a lace or silk stole complete the costume.

Figure 57   Regency ball-gown, after Lawrence (c. 1812)

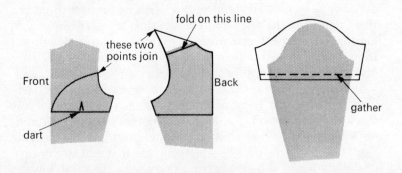

Figure 58   Diagram for Fig. 57

Figures 59 and 60   Gown with 'gigot' sleeves, 1832

This is an elaborate gown, but so attractive as to be worth time spent in the making. The finished effect should be dainty and summery, and curtain net with a Vandyke patterned border would be ideal. The bodice and facings should be in satin or taffeta, in a pastel shade, the flounced net overskirt being mounted on a matching petticoat. As with any of these off-the-shoulder styles, the bodice needs to be lined and boned, and must fit tightly.

Modify the basic bodice pattern as indicated in *figure 60*. Insert boning in back bodice along the seam lines and leave a centre back opening. (I am fully aware that the mere suggestion of zippers sets the purists shuddering. But no harassed *amateur* wardrobe mistress or dresser has time to fiddle with the complicated authenticity of hooks and loops, so I remain unrepentant.)

Cut a straight strip of the bodice material 5 in (13 cm) wide, and sufficient in length to fit round the dropped neckline (just below the point of the shoulder)—about 38–42 in (97–107 cm) depending on the breadth of shoulders. This links back and front bodice together across the upper arm, at the same time serving as a band into which the frills and tops of sleeves can be set. The sleeve is a much exaggerated version of the Renaissance sleeve at *figure 48* and needs to be interlined with iron-on Vilene, to get the puffed effect.

The ruche across the bodice can be of net, cut from the plain 'left overs' from the frills, which will use up a considerable amount of border. Curtain net can usually be bought in varying depths, with the same border design, so if a 36 in (1 m) width is used, this will leave ample from which to cut the ballooning top sections.

Fold under the top 4 in (10 cm) of the sleeve head (just above the matching notches) of the basic paper pattern, and cut a plain sleeve from the bodice fabric, and take in till a smooth fit over the forearm is achieved. Before sewing underarm seam, mark a line below the elbow, about $\frac{2}{3}$ from wrist (as in diagram). Gather the lower edge of net oversleeve, and with right sides together, match to this line, and machine. This utilizes the top of the sleeve as a lining, and eliminates an extra thickness.

Figure 59   Gown with 'gigot' sleeves, 1832

Gather the top of the net oversleeve to the same size as under-sleeve at armhole, and baste the two sections together. The undersleeve will probably need a little gathering to make it fit snugly across the upper arm. Join armhole sections below matching notches, to back and front bodice, but do not close underarm sleeve seams or bodice side seams yet—it is easier to work flat than struggle with gathers in the round.

Take the measurement across the back neckline, over the shoulders, and down over the bust to the waist. (Average about 54 in (137 cm). The top frill is fairly narrow (about 3½ in (9 cm)) and is made of the bodice material. Allow about 2 yds

(190 cm) for this, and trim to a point at each end. *Note:* On account of the back fastening, these frills must be cut at centre back, but the fullness will conceal this—the edges should be finished with very narrow roll hems.

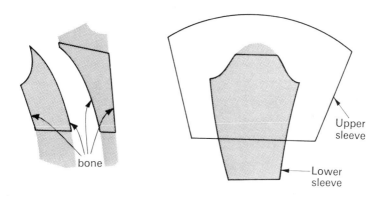

Figure 60   Diagram for Fig. 59

For each frill (before halving for back opening) allow twice the measurement mentioned at the beginning of the previous paragraph, i.e. about 3 yds (2·75 m) each. If this is considered too expensive, the number of frills can be reduced to two without losing too much effect. Layer the frills—say 12–9–6 in (30–23–15 cm) and baste edges together, tapering the front to nothing. (It is much easier to do this in one operation—when completed, the frills can be pulled apart.) Draw up gathers until the correct fit is obtained across the back, over the shoulders and down over bust to waist. For ease of handling, lay a narrow tape, Paris binding or shoulder strap ribbon over the gathering line of all three or four frills, and machine together. Baste along back of neck, over sleeve head and down front of *side* bodice. Arrange ruche across the top of the centre front panel and secure with concealed tacks to hold folds in place. With right sides together, pin and baste front to side fronts, sandwiching the frills from armhole down to waist. Machine firmly. Bone side seams, and put shortened bones at side front seams (as far as under-bust—see diagram). Bone also at centre front.

Machine a straight strip about $1\frac{1}{2}$ in (4 cm) wide, down centre front and trim with ornamental buttons.

Baste the long straight strip of material all round neckline, fold in half, and slip-stitch over all raw edges.

Make a full-length waist slip in taffeta lining fabric; make the lower frill about the length from just above knee to ground; gather and machine firmly to under-petticoat. Make upper skirt to just below knee; gather and adjust to waist measurement; machine to under-petticoat. Join skirt to bodice, and finish off with a sash of contrasting colour.

For the method of making the bonnet see *Stage Costumes and How to Make Them*.

Figures 61 and 62   Day dress (c 1875)

This gown is taken from a photograph of my grandmother. I cannot date it exactly, but she was born in 1855, and in the photograph she appears to be in her twenties. She was a lady's maid, and so would probably have had considerable fashion sense. This was probably her 'best' dress, and appears to be in a darkish, dull-surfaced material, trimmed with ribbon ruching. It might have been worn over a small crinoline, or possibly a bustle, but nothing exaggerated. A good quality gown, suitable for a middle-class housewife.

For stage wear, it could be carried out in a variety of fabrics, depending on season, age of character etc. It is very simple in cut, and the period effect relies entirely on the trimming.

The bodice is cut from the basic pattern, with a slightly dropped shoulder line, as indicated in *figure 62*. The basic sleeve is cut to three-quarter length, and slightly wider, to accommodate the undersleeve, which is a deep, buttoned cuff attached to the sleeve lining. The front of the bodice is filled in with a tucked gilet. The neck is set into a narrow band, topped with a frill. The lappets terminate in pockets, cut as in *figure 62*. Make a narrow hem along straight edge; run a double gathering thread $1\frac{1}{4}$ in (3 cm) from the edge, draw up to fit across lappet; machine gathers into position, and trim stitch-line with a contrast piping. Attach to curved end of lappet. Make up a continuous length of ruching sufficient to edge both lappets and to trim bodice as in sketch—the ruche

Figure 61   Day dress (c. 1875)

will extend across the back of the bodice, across the shoulders.
Sew ruche to edges of lappets, which should be lined and should
hang loose from the waist as in drawing.

The skirt is fairly full; the front is cut in one piece, and the
back can have a centre seam. Use basic flared pattern, enlarged
as necessary. Make a flounce about 10 in (25 cm) deep, and
attach to lower edge. The skirt trim is a straight piece of
matching material about 7 in (18 cm) wide and twice the lower
edge measurement. Set in 1 in (2·5 cm) pleats at lower edge—
(just covering the seam of the frill), then set in pleats at the top
edge, but reversing the direction, so that each pleat-edge is
slightly twisted. Add single ruches of ribbon top and bottom,
and cover edges with a contrast piping. It is easier to carry out
all these operations before joining the back seam.

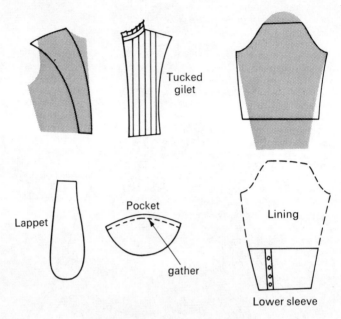

Figure 62   Diagram for Fig. 61

Finally, join skirt to bodice, taking in the lappet ends as shown in the drawing.

Figures 63 and 64   Ball-gown, 1879

It is difficult to see how one could have danced at all in the gowns of this period—presumably one either took no more than a mincing step, or just stood around looking elegant. One certainly would hardly dare to sit down in a 'cuirasse' bodice.

This must be cut in eight sections, and the basic pattern does not really suffice. It is better to select a panelled style, having seams centre back and front, and side back and front. The bodice is made separately from the skirt. Cut it long enough to fit well below the waist, extending about 2 in (5 cm) below the wearer's hip bone, bringing the lower edge almost to the crease of the thigh when the wearer sits down. Centre front and centre back may be brought to a shallow point, as indicated in *figure 64*. Line and interline the bodice, and a better fit is obtained by boning the seams.

Figure 63   Ball-gown, 1879

Cut the underskirt with the minimum of fulness, and dart to fit smoothly at waist and hips. Cut with a centre back seam and do not close this seam until the overskirt has been ruched on to it. (It is always easier to work on a flat section.) Measure and mark three basting or chalked lines—the first just above the knee, the second below the knee and the third equidistant from the second—about 9 in (23 cm) apart is a good average. Cut the overskirt about 9 in (23 cm) longer than the underskirt, and about one-and-a-half times the width. Dart at waist (back and front) and at hips, to dispose of extra fullness. From lower hem, measure and mark the same distance as the lowest line on the underskirt, and run double gathering threads. Run another pair of threads about 11½ in (29 cm) above this line, and a third pair equidistant above this line. Draw up threads carefully to fit underskirt, and match each set of gathers to marked lines on underskirt. Machine each set of gathers to underskirt, and trim each ruche with a contrasting ribbon, possibly of the same material as the bodice.

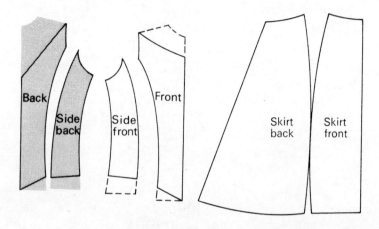

Figure 64   Diagram for Fig. 63

A swathe of the same material as the bodice, cut on the bias, and with a lace flounce is draped round the hips and fastened under the train, which must not be so long as to be unwieldy—it need not trail for more than about 18 in (46 cm). It is a long straight piece of the bodice material, gathered and bunched at the back, and fastened firmly to the back of the bodice. An effective method is to contrive a very large bow, and then catch the 'tails' together to complete the train.

The actual bustle worn with this gown, and with the next costume described, should not be the exaggerated 'bird cage' of the later period, but a smallish kidney-shaped pad tied round the waist—just sufficient to lift the skirt and enhance the impression of a very small waist.

Contrasting textures of fabric make this an interesting gown, one which I can see in rich chestnut satin for the bodice and train, with a skirt of delicate pink nylon, ruched on to heavy poult in crushed strawberry pink. If the train were lined with similar poult, it would give the authentic rustle.

Figure 65   Walking dress, 1880

Figures 65 and 66   Walking dress, 1880

This follows the same lines as the previous costume, except that the front has faced lapels, and sleeves are added. Much the same method of cutting is followed, though the front is cut to a deeper point (*figure 66*). The chief problem with the bodice section is the fastening—probably in the original a multitude of tiny hooks and loops anchoring the jacket to a gilet. Though the purists may shudder, I suggest a carefully concealed, fine, open-ended zipper fastening to just above the waist. The draped pannier can be attached to the lower edge of the bodice, and should be cut on the bias, as indicated in the diagram. It is softly pleated at the back and front points, and the bodice lining is then turned in and slip-stitched over the raw edges.

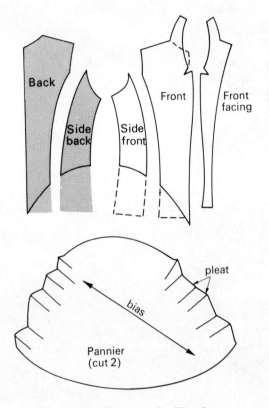

Figure 66   Diagram for Fig. 65

The skirt is in two sections—the underskirt, which can be made of thin taffeta or rayon, to eliminate bulk, has two deep flounces of the main material. The overskirt is a little fuller, to allow for being caught up to display the flounces. Extra richness can be achieved by piping the lapels with velvet and banding the lower edge of the jacket to match. The front of the jacket is filled in with a contrasting gilet, frilled at the neck.

Figures 67 and 68   Day dress, 1899

This is another example of a 'period' effect very easily achieved. It is suitable for, say *The Cherry Orchard* or any play set at the turn of the century.

The bolero jacket is cut from the basic bodice pattern, modified as in *figure 68*. The close-fitting sleeve is only slightly puffed, as shown in diagram.

For the skirt, use the 'standard' pattern, modified as in diagram.

Figure 67   Day dress, 1899

The trimming can be achieved in various ways. One method is to lay a matching strip and machine rows of top-stitching as in drawing. Alternatively, top stitch a contrasting strip. Or use a lighter-weight contrast—say a dull satin on a dress-weight woollen, and pad lightly with a single layer of wadding before stitching. As a complete contrast, trim with three rows of bias-cut rouleau, stitched on by hand. This means considerably

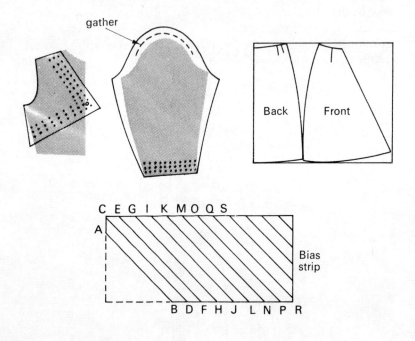

Figure 68   Diagram for Fig. 67

more work, but is very effective. To make the rouleau, a continuous length of bias-cut material is necessary, entailing the joining of a number of such strips. There is a method of doing this which simplifies matters considerably, and can effect economies by utilizing the cuttings.

Square off the longer edges of a rectangle by pulling parallel threads. Trim one short edge on the true bias, as in *figure 68*. From this edge measure and mark on the wrong side of the fabric the desired width of the bias strip. Measure and mark the same distance from this line, and continue thus to the end of the fabric (the last line will probably run out on the short edge but this does not matter). These markings should be taken right to the edge of the fabric, and must be clear and accurate, as they will form the cutting line. Now, with right side inside, fold strip in half and match point B to point C, point D to point E,

point F to point G and so on. Pin carefully, setting pins about
$\frac{1}{8}$ in (3 cm) from the edge. *Note:* This is not a dead straight
fold, and the fabric will 'wring' slightly, but this instruction
must be observed, and each point must be matched exactly,
otherwise the operation fails. In actual fact, the narrower the
strip, the more the edges will 'fight' and a 4 in (10 cm) strip is
about the workable minimum. Machine along the pinned edges,
using a fine stitch. If the material is inclined to fray, go back and
overlock edges with swing-needle.

You now have a tube of material with a spiral seam. Point A
will form an 'ear' at one end. Hold this in the left hand and
slide your fingers into the tube to hold it open and taut. Starting
at point B, cut carefully along the marked lines, which should
all in turn meet at the seam. This will give you a long bias-cut
strip. Press seams all in the same direction.

It is quite surprising how much emerges from a small piece
of material utilized in this manner. My own experiment was
made with a piece of cotton material 4 in × 33 in (10 cm × 84
cm) marked out with a $1\frac{1}{8}$ in (2·75 cm) ruler. This gave a continuous bias strip of about 98 in (250 cm), from what was
virtually useless waste. Two yards of new material, utilized as
indicated in diagram, would yield a 3 in (7·5 cm) strip (after
turnings) of about 32 yd.

To convert into a rouleau, fold the strip in half and machine
edges together, using a fine stitch and taking the minimum
turning (on a very narrow rouleau, no more than one-third of
the finished width). When machining, pull the material gently
towards you, so that the seam is not too tight. If a machine with
attachments is available, use the disc recommended for stretch
seams. At the ends of the seam, run back a few stitches, then
forward, before cutting cotton. Take a fine safety-pin, fasten it
through the seam allowance at the end of the tube (making sure
that all the little seams lie away from pin), tuck the head
inside tube, and gradually work it until the raw edge is drawn
inwards. Work pin through the tube, taking care not to strain
and break the sewing thread. When completely turned, run
thumb-nail along the seam, but do not iron, as this flattens
rouleaux.

Rouleaux can be used for a variety of costumes—frogging or
braiding can be made from it, as can ornamental points.

Figure 69   Pre-1914 suit with 'hobble' skirt

Figures 69 and 70   Pre-1914 suit with 'hobble' skirt

The 'hobble skirt' of the years just preceding the First World War was in fact just that—women minced and hobbled, and had to be helped on and off buses. For practical stage wear, the skirt need not be so exaggeratedly narrow, though the lower hem should not exceed the wearer's hip measurement. As bulk must be eliminated, it is preferable to line the skirt and dispense with an underslip.

The skirt is simple in cut, having a 1-piece back and a 2-piece front, the right front modified as in diagram. The extra

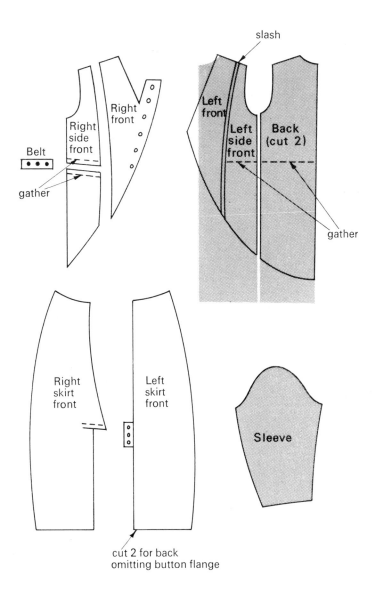

Figure 70   Diagram for Fig. 69

fullness is gathered and secured under a 3-button tab which takes up the theme of the half-belt of the jacket.

For the jacket, use the basic sheath-line dress. As this will need more modification than can be achieved merely by folding, it is better to cut a replica in newspaper. Slash the back as indicated in diagram, and trim away as shown, to fit in to the waist (*figure 70*). (When using 'slashed' patterns, always allow for turnings at the points where cuts have been made.) Make a corresponding slash in front section. Slash side front at waist, and modify to allow for slight extra fullness, which is gathered under buttoned half-belt similar to skirt tab. Cut left front as indicated in diagram, and finish with a facing which can be taken back to the seam. The right front is extended to button across on to the left front, as indicated in diagram. This section is also faced back to the seam.

The sleeve is plain, and can be cut either from the basic pattern, or from a 2-piece sleeve pattern, without modification.

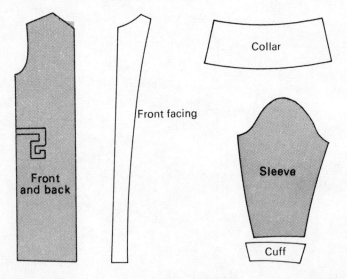

Figure 71   Diagram for Fig. 72

Figures 71 and 72   Fur trimmed coat, 1927

This coat, cut simply and without exaggeration, is very typical of its date. It can be made directly from the basic plain sheath

Figure 72 Fur-trimmed coat, 1927

pattern, making only a slight modification for the extra facing, which can be cut in one with the front (*figure 71*). The trimming can be of contrasting wide braid on the lapels and on the lower front. The original model would have had pockets, but unless the script calls for these specifically, the extra work involved is hardly necessary.

As a variant, the same style can be made in light-weight material, omitting the fur collar and cuffs, in which case the collar is simply a straight piece of material.

The cloche hat had a high crown, sometimes crushed at the top, and a very narrow brim. This style can be evolved from a felt hood, cutting away the brim to about 2 in (5 cm). A V-shaped section cut out on the left side will give the right fit to the turn-up, and the rest of the brim is trimmed down to about 1 in (2·5 cm).

SLEEVE VARIATIONS

Figure 73   Virago sleeve, 1600s

This is an interesting and easily contrived sleeve which can transform a plain gown into a 'period piece' with the minimum of trouble and expense. It was fashionable early in the reign of Charles I and possibly it was imported from France by his queen, Henrietta Maria. Reference to contemporary Stuart portraiture shows that the style lasted upwards of thirty years, though its appearance as late as 1662 may have been the kind of 'second-time-round' which seems to occur.

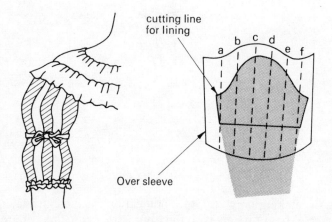

Figure 73   Virago sleeve, 1600s, with diagram

Using the basic sleeve pattern, enlarged as in *figure 73*, cut main sleeve and slash into seven pieces, as indicated by the broken lines. Interline the five centre strips with Vilene or other non-woven stiffening. The quickest way to do this is to mark out the main sleeve and lay it on the Vilene, then work a row of plain or zig-zag stitching on either side of the marked line, ½ in (1 cm) from the lines b, c, d and e, but only one row of stitching at lines a and f. Cut along markings, taking care to keep the strips in the right order. The two underarm pieces will be unstiffened.

Cut six contrasting strips of approximately the same width as the main ones, and insert between main strips. Pleat under at armhole and lower edge, just above elbow. Catch together the pieces of the main sleeve at these points and gather slightly at armhole and lower edge—this is a three-quarter length sleeve. Mount the whole sleeve on a close fitting lining, finish underarm seam, and trim lower edge with a double lace frill. Gather at the intermediate point with a contrasting ribbon tied in a bow.

Figure 74   Flounced sleeve, mid-1700s

The rather casual sleeves of the Restoration gave place to a plain, close-fitting elbow-length sleeve, and for this, the basic sleeve, trimmed to the appropriate length, can be used. Various trimmings can be added. The basic sleeve may be cut slightly fuller and finished with a broad, stiffened cuff, under which hangs a lawn or lace frill.

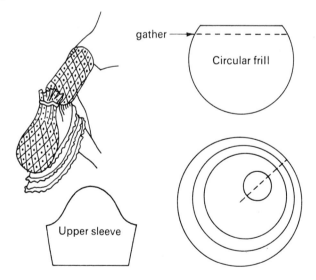

Figure 74   Flounced sleeve, mid 1700s, with diagram

The very attractive sleeve illustrated is shown in a 1750 portrait of a young lady in a sack-back gown. The upper sleeve is plain and quite close fitting, and from the elbow falls a matching circular frill, from which a segment has been cut away and the straight edge gathered to the main sleeve as shown in the sketch. Beneath this are three flounces of lace-edged lawn. These are simple to contrive, and consist merely of three concentric circles of varying depth. Cut the first circle with a 12 in (30 cm) radius, the second 10 in (26 cm) and the third 8 in (20 cm). Edge with 2 in (5 cm) lace. (There is no need to pleat this any more than will allow it to lie flat.) Place the circles one on top of the other and pin firmly round the circumference. Mark on the diameter—but off-centre as indicated in diagram —a circle having a circumference slightly larger than the arm measurement taken just above the elbow, say 12–14 in (30–35 cm). A rule of thumb method to cut this circle is to divide the circumference by six, which gives the approximate radius of the circle to be cut away. If the resultant edge is slightly larger than the sleeve edge, it can be gathered; if it is too small, trim away a little more. Baste the three circles together, attach to sleeve with right sides together, oversew or bind raw edges. If the sleeve is lined, slip-stitch lining over raw edges.

This portrait also shows the young lady wearing a *bergere* hat over a small cap of lace-edged lawn. The hat can be made from a wide-brimmed fine straw (panama, leghorn, bankok) with a very shallow crown, round which is a looped ribbon and bow. Strings are attached under the brim and tied, not under the chin, but at the nape of the neck. The brim, according to a fashion of the day, must be turned up back and front.

The same type of sleeve is shown in another portrait of 1756, but instead of the triple *lawn* frill, it has three scalloped matching frills, and only one lawn frill. However, the same method of making would apply.

Figures 75 and 76 Beret and imbecile sleeves, 1830–40

The Beret sleeve is almost like a Tam o' Shanter bonnet with a hole in the top. Cut the sleeve in two sections, as indicated in diagram, and interline with Vilene. Mount on a plain, very

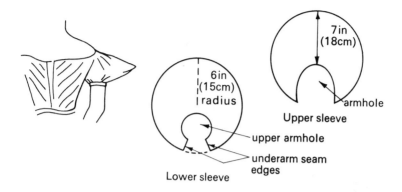

Figure 75   Beret sleeve (c. 1830), with diagram

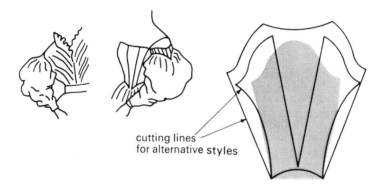

Figure 76   Imbecile sleeve (c. 1836), with diagram

short inner sleeve and finish off with a narrow band round the upper arm.

The 'Imbecile' sleeve was a version of the leg-of-mutton, very much exaggerated. Cut the plain sleeve pattern from shoulder to wrist, and extend it as shown in *figure 76*. The wider the two sections are spread, the larger the sleeve will be. Mount on a Vilene interlining, and if using flimsy material, use the iron-on type, as this is thinner.

This sleeve should fit closely at the lower forearm, or may have a deep, tight-fitting cuff.

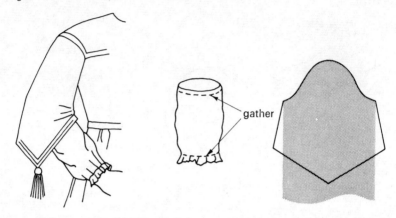

Figure 77   Pagoda sleeve, with 'engageants'

Figure 77   Pagoda sleeve, with 'engageants'

This was worn about 1857, and was a two-piece sleeve with a contrasting undersleeve—the 'engageant'. The upper sleeve is cut from the wide sleeve pattern, modified to three-quarter length and coming to a point, as indicated in *figure 77*. The undersleeve is made in contrasting material, and need only reach to just above the elbow, where it is held in place by elastic.

CHAPTER SIX

AMERICANA

In discussing American costume, the diversity of dress in a country with so many influences may cause the writer to settle for *Gone with the Wind, Showboat*, and the determinedly persistent Western and American Indian. The play costumer may rely on the ignorance of the audience as to the difference between Sioux and Apache, and can safely take a broad brush.

A detailed description of American historical costume may be found in *Five Centuries of American Costume*, by R. Turner Wilcox, an indispensable book for those requiring meticulous authenticity. However, its very exhaustiveness can be a stumbling block, as to use it the designer must know, for instance, which particular British regiment was engaged in any particular fight, or which tribe of American Indians attacked the stockade on a certain date. To my mind the important thing is the drama and the overall impression. The following handful of costumes emerges as the minimum requirement to this end.

Composite American Indian
Western cowboy
Frontiersman
Settlers: Puritan and later (westward trek)
Soldiers: British and American (War of Independence)
　　　　　Union and Confederate (Civil War)

For the rest, people on both sides of the Atlantic dressed pretty much the same. George Washington would have looked very little different from an English country gentleman; Abraham Lincoln could have passed for a rugged midland industrialist of the 1860s.

Fashion did not take a one-way ticket to the New World, and at least three indispensable items have crossed from America to Europe. Many a home dressmaker has blessed the memory of Ebenezer Butterick who, in 1863 (in Sterling, Massachusetts), cut for his wife the paper pattern of a shirt, and so laid the foundation of a craft which has smoothed the path of needlewomen the world over. Levi Strauss certainly started something when he devised the blue denim pants still known as 'Levis'. And what dressmaker hasn't at some time or another treadled away at a Singer sewing machine?

Figures 78 and 79   American Indian

The generally accepted costume for the American Indian, in a production which does not specifically identify the tribe, is a 'breech-clout' consisting of two small aprons, one back and one front, hanging from a leather belt and worn over a loin cloth. The width of the breech-clout should be about one-third of the waist measurement, and the length about two-thirds the waist to knee measurement.

A more elaborate costume would consist of a buckskin tunic and leggings. The American Indians were highly skilled in making clothing from animal skins, and although skins or leather would be far too expensive, these can be imitated by using felt of a suitable colour. This material has the added advantage of being easy to cut into fringe and it does not fray.

American Indian women can also wear the fringed tunic, banded with braid, and with black wool tufts to imitate scalp-locks.

The American Indians made extensive use of feathers, which had a very special significance, depending on species and number, each feather denoting some particular deed. These can be worn in combination with a braid or beaded headband, and the elaborate traditional feather headdress worn by an American Indian Chief can also be made on a braid foundation.

Real feathers are expensive, and if the costumes are for short-term use, feathers can be made from painted buckram or even stout paper. Cut a pattern of the required length and width, in imitation of a large quill (see *figure 79*) paint it the required colour, using a bird book for reference. Buckram will have to be damped, to eliminate its tendency to curl. Mark the centre vein on the feather and use pinking shears to cut to the required shape. This gives a sharply defined, regular notch for cutting, and by cutting evenly down each notch to within about a quarter inch of the centre line, a very convincing feather is created. Make the centre spine firm by using millinery wire

Figure 78   American Indian

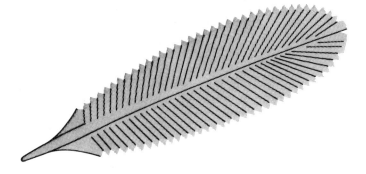

Figure 79   Buckram feather

Figure 80   Cowboy

attached with herringbone stitches. If paper is used, cut two thicknesses, and before cutting, gum them together with the wire spine sandwiched in between. Long, paper-covered wires (plant ties) could be used, and these would stick more easily.

Figures 80 and 81   Cowboy

General information on what the cowboy wore may be gathered from any television 'western'. The indispensables are a 10-gallon 'cowboy' hat, and 'chaps' (*chaparajos*) or leggings. The hat is easy; use any large, floppy hat, with a deep dent in the crown, with the wide brim steamed to the desired curve and shape. The edge may be bound with narrow grosgrain ribbon, or with braid, and millinery wire may be threaded through the ribbon to make it easy to shape the brim.

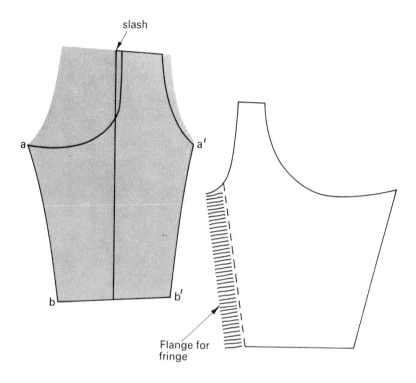

Figure 81   Diagram for chaparajos

Use the pyjama trouser pattern for the 'chaps', modified as in *figure 81*. As these 'chaps' have no inner-leg seam, fold the original pattern in half, slash and reposition as shown in the diagram, trimming away the marked portion.

A variety of material may be used—fur fabric, to look like sheepskin, or any type of imitation leather. The rest of the costume—Levis, a checked shirt, with a brightly coloured neckerchief—presents no problem. A suède or cloth vest cut from the pyjama-top pattern adds variety, though ready-made vests will do.

Figures 82 and 83   Frontiersman

The frontiersman costume is hybrid in style, and is adapted from

Figure 82   Frontiersman

the American Indian 'wamus', a skin tunic, fringed at the lower edge and trimmed with fringe across the yoke, down the sleeve, and at the collar edge. Use the basic pattern, and slash as indicated in *figure 83*. Allow about 3 or 4 in (8–10 cm) at the points indicated, and mark this fringe allowance on the wrong side of the fabric. Position the other section at this mark, leaving the fringe allowance as a loose flange on the right side. Seam the two sections together with a flat seam, then cut the flange into fringe—this is easier than fringing first, as the tails might then get caught in the seam.

The collar is a straight piece, fringed on the two short and one long edges; the neck opening is laced with a leather thong.

The coonskin hat of the Davy Crockett type may be made from fur if available, otherwise fur fabric may be used.

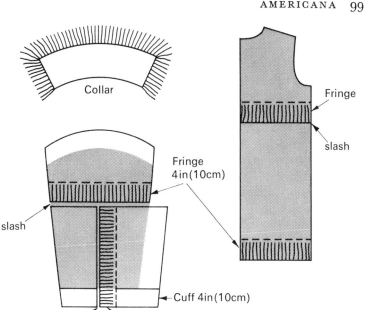

Collar

Fringe

slash

Fringe
4in(10cm)

slash

Cuff 4in(10cm)

slash   Fringe

Figure 83   Diagram for 'wamus' (fringed tunic)

Settlers of various nationalities brought their own styles of dress with them to America, and it would be impossible to depict them all.

Many of the early colonists from England were Puritans, whose garb would be devoid of ornament and sober in colour. In cut it follows the styles of the first half of the seventeenth century, but with all slashing and braiding eliminated. Breeches may be made in the same way as the 'slops' for which instructions are given in the chapter on English Variations, using dark, homespun textures in place of satin. The jacket is simple and plain; use the pyjama-jacket pattern, cut fairly long— about midway between waist and knee. Leave the side seams open at the bottom for about 12 in (30 cm). Finish off with a plain-white linen collar and matching cuffs.

The hat is of black felt, high-crowned, and with a straight brim. This can be contrived by steaming and ironing an old fedora, or by cutting down the brim of a bought floppy hat.

The Puritan woman's dress is equally severe: a plain, close-fitting bodice, high in the neck, with a cape-like falling collar and plain white cuffs. The skirt is straight, and is gathered at the waist. No hoop or hip-pad was worn.

Her hairstyle was severe, and was concealed beneath a cap, tied under the chin with strings. This cap may be a modification of the mob cap. The crown is a circle large enough to cover the head, but instead of the frill, it is finished off with a straight turned-back band to frame the face. Alternatively, the plain bonnet at *figure 113* may be used, and the band added to that.

Later, on the westward trek, women's dresses were made of gingham or rough cotton of the homespun type, cut in shirtwaist style, with full skirts gathered and set into tight-fitting waistbands. Extra fullness may be achieved by using the standard pattern in *figure 43*.

Figures 84 and 85 Sunbonnet

The cotton sunbonnet which women wore was an adaptation of the eighteenth-century calash, but overall much smaller, except that the front and neck frills were wider, to provide adequate shade. The cut is simple, as in *figure 85*. Take the head measurement (round the forehead) and divide the figure by four, to obtain the width of the back panel. For example, a 22 in (56 cm) head measurement when divided by four gives $5\frac{1}{4}$ in (14 cm), which includes a $\frac{5}{8}$ in (1 cm) seam allowance, leaving a finished width of 4 in (10 cm). To make a pattern, cut a rectangle of paper $5\frac{1}{2}$ in (15 cm) $\times 7\frac{1}{2}$ in (19 cm). Fold the long sides together, mark 2 in (5 cm) from top outer corner; round off the corners to the fold. At lower corner, mark $\frac{3}{4}$ in (2 cm) and trim away in a soft curve, as indicated in diagram. Open out and cut two pieces to this pattern.

The crown and brim is one straight piece 36 × 12 in (1 m × 31 cm). Make a narrow hem on one long side (a–b). From this hem measure $3\frac{1}{2}$ in (9 cm) and mark a line (c–d). Mark three more lines spaced 2 in (5 cm) apart (e–f; g–h; i–j). Fold at line c–d and sandwich a piece of nylon string inside this fold. Baste or pin close to the string, and using the cording or zipper foot attachment on the sewing machine, run a line of stitching close to the string. This is, in effect, a tuck through which is threaded

Figure 84   Sunbonnet

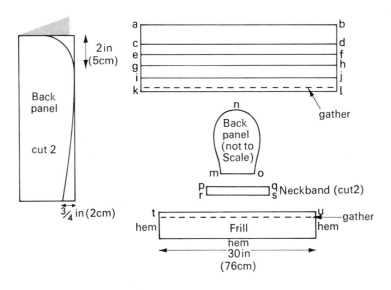

Figure 85   Diagram for sunbonnet

a gathering cord. The tuck needs to be slightly less than $\frac{1}{4}$ in ($\frac{1}{2}$ cm), and I found in practice that it was too narrow to take a bodkin or threader carrying the string, so the string had to be inserted first. It may, in fact, be found easier to run this line of stitching by hand.

Tie a knot in the string at point (c), and leave a tail of string about 2 in at point (d). Repeat the tuck operation along the lines e–f, g–h, and i–j. Now run gathering threads at the edge k–l. By running double threads along this edge, it makes the gathers easier to control. Alternatively, a machine ruffler attachment can be used, if it is adjusted to the correct stitch length.

Draw up the threads along this line, k–l, reducing it to about 16 in (41 cm) to fit the back panel at the edge marked m—n—o. Space out the gathers evenly; pin the gathered edge to the curved edge of the panel, baste and machine together. Press the raw edges inwards. Turn under the seam allowance on the second panel and baste; match this panel over the raw edges, m–n–o, and slip-stitch into place.

Draw up the strings at points (b), (d), (f), (h), and (j) so that the bonnet fits snugly over the head; about 18 in (46 cm). Knot the string to prevent slipping, and adjust the gathers. It will be found that a better brim will be achieved if fewer gathers are set in the centre 9 in (23 cm) and the surplus fullness is drawn down at each side.

Make very narrow hems at edges a–c and b–d, and pin small pleats at points (e), (g) and (i) so that the lower edge fits the neck. Cut two strips 12 in (31 cm) × 1$\frac{1}{2}$ in (4 cm), and one strip 30 × 5 in (76 cm × 13 cm). Make narrow hems along the short edges and along one long edge of the latter. Gather and draw up to fit neck (about 11 in). Sandwich the gathered edge between the two 12-in strips at points r–s, and machine together. Press strips upwards.

With right sides together, pin or baste the edge of *one* strip p–q to the neck edge of the bonnet (points c, m–o, d). Machine the two sections together, then press all raw edges inwards. Turn under the seam allowance of the free neck strip, and lap this over the raw edges at neck edge and slip-stitch into position. Make narrow bonnet strings; tuck one into each open end of the neckband at points p–r and q–s. Stitch firmly.

Figure 86   Schoolmarm, or housewife

A character who appears regularly in westerns is the girl in the saloon. She must wear fancy, gaudy clothes of the appropriate period, with an exaggerated décolletage, an elegant cut, and a perfect fit. The corseted look of the 'cuirasse' outfits of the late 1870s and early 1880s, as shown in the chapter on English Variations is suitable.

Figures 86 and 87

A less elaborate costume would be worn by a housewife or schoolmarm. The dress at *figure 86*, of about 1825, gives some idea of the type. The close-fitting bodice is cut almost off the shoulder, with a deep V-line, and the yoke is filled in with tucked muslin or lawn, finished with a standing frilled collar. Modify the basic pattern as in *figure 87*, and use the puffed sleeve described in the Renaissance chapter at *figure 48*. Use the standard pattern for the skirt (*figure 43*). A plain white linen apron, covering the front of the skirt, is also suitable. This gown can be made in a plain dark fabric, but the same method can be used to make a summer dress, using gingham, cotton, etc.

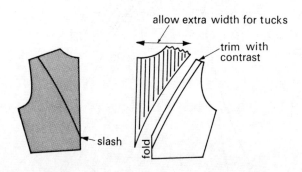

allow extra width for tucks

trim with contrast

slash

fold

Figure 87   Diagram for Fig. 86 (bodice)

Military costumes are not easy to contrive, and for a full-scale adult production, renting may be preferable. However, for school plays, this may not be practicable, on account of both cost and sizing.

The highlights in this field are, of course, the American Revolutionary period, and the Civil War. As regards the former, a very wide choice exists, since uniforms were not standardized, nor did they differ widely from civilian garb, except in so far as accoutrements were concerned. Reference books and military museums will provide information on detail should this be required.

Figure 88   American soldier and British soldier

Basically, the uniforms of both armies can be reduced to a common denominator: headgear, jacket, and breeches. The latter were close fitting, and buttoned just below the knee. They were worn with white stockings and buckled shoes, and some-

Figure 88 American and British soldiers, War of Independence

times with 'spatterdashes' or leggings. These latter reached either to the knees, or halfway up the calf.

Figure 89 Uniform breeches

Cut the breeches from the pyjama pattern, modified as in *figure 89*. For younger wearers, they can be finished off at the waist with either a waistband, or with elastic inserted in a casing. For adults and teenagers, the breeches can be made with

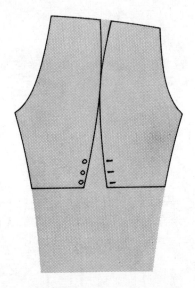

Figure 89   Diagram for uniform breeches

a flap opening; they did not have a fly front, and fitted fairly closely at the hips.

Figure 90   'Spatterdashes' or leggings

The leggings can be made by the same method as described for the buskins in the Accessories chapter, but instead of a front lacing, they are seamed down the front of the leg and instep, and buttoned down the outside leg. To save work, and to speed up dressing, the buttons may be sewn on and the leggings fastened by means of a concealed zipper. Cut as in *figure 90*, from close-woven woollen fabric, denim, duck, linen, felt, or Vinyl—the latter will simulate leather. Finish off with an elastic strap under the instep.

Figure 91   Uniform jacket

Cut the jacket from the basic pattern, modified as in *figure 91*. The facings are important, so is the lining, as both these sections show, and the variations in colour denote different regiments. It

Figure 90   *'Spatterdashes,' or leggings*

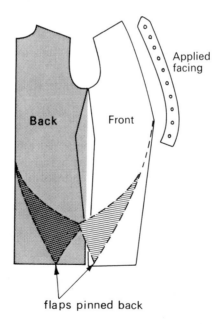

Figure 91   *Diagram for uniform jacket*

is easier to apply the front facing before making up the jacket.

Where epaulettes are appropriate, make these from buckram covered with fabric or felt. To make the fringe, use either thick string, rug wool or several strands of double-knitting wool. Take a length slightly more than double the length required, anchor one end firmly (under the case of the sewing machine, in a doorjamb or a table drawer); twist tightly until the strand forms a tight little skein. Tie the ends to prevent unravelling. Make up enough skeins to fit round the end of the epaulette and sew firmly in place. Paint either gold or silver, as appropriate; some regiments did, in fact, wear red or green epaulettes, and these can be made from coloured wool, which twists and skeins easily.

Colour information must be obtained from reference books, as the variations are too numerous to list. In general, it is fairly safe to use dark blue for the American uniforms, and red for the British. This is not to say that all the American regiments did in fact wear blue, nor that the Redcoats always wore red. But it avoids confusion in the mind of the audience.

Both armies wore the tails of the coat buttoned back, showing the lining, and because the fronts were cut away, waistcoats or vests will be necessary, but these need only be fronts attached at the side seams and armholes.

Figure 92   Tricorne and mitre helmet

Headgear, broadly, falls into two categories: the tricorne which resulted from pinning up the broad brim of the Cavalier hat; and the high, pointed mitre emanating from the continent of Europe. The former, invariably black, was common to both American and British. It may be plain, or with braided edges, and again, the floppy felt serves admirably.

The mitre helmet evolved from the stocking cap. A high, shaped front-piece was added on which was superimposed the embroidered or metal insignia. Later the tip of the cap was attached to the peak of the front piece.

Cut the front from buckram, wide enough to fit across the forehead, and as high as the measurement from hair-line to chin. Make the cap section from felt, cut as in the diagram. Mount the cap and front-piece on a close-fitting headband of

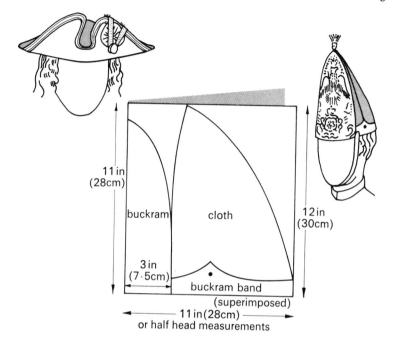

Figure 92   Tricorne and mitre helmet

grosgrain ribbon. Paint the insignia in the appropriate colours, silver, gold, etc.

Figures 93, 94 and 95   Union and Confederate soldiers

By the time the Civil War broke out, uniforms had been standardized. The Union Army (*figure 93*) wore dark blue and the Confederate Army (*figure 94*) wore gray, but the cut was similar. Use the basic pattern, modified as indicated in *figure 95*. The officers' jackets were longer than those of the non-commissioned ranks.

The Union Army officers wore wide-brimmed black hats, cocked on the left side. The non-commissioned officers and other ranks wore military kepis, with a leather peak, and the Confederate army wore the same type of cap, but in gray.

Figure 93   Union soldier   *Figure 94   Confederate soldier*

Figure 96   Kepi

Cut the kepi as at *figure 96*. The crown can be thin felt or cloth, and the peak any kind of shiny, simulated leather, or stick-on Contact. Stiffen the circular top with buckram or cardboard, and interline the headband. Finish off with the chin strap and badge.

Since so many plays of the Civil War period include the Negro slave in the cast the appropriate costume must be included here. The male slave may wear any tattered trousers, a shabby or torn shirt, and a wide-brimmed, battered straw hat.

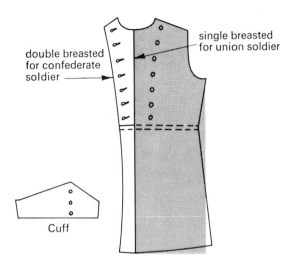

Figure 95   Diagram for uniform jacket

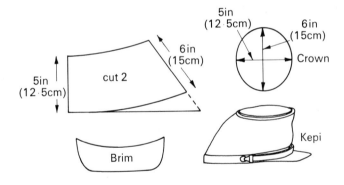

Figure 96   Kepi

Female slaves may wear full-skirted cotton dresses, gathered at the waist. Their heads are covered with cotton kerchiefs—a square about 36 in (I m) folded into a triangle and tied 'mammy' fashion, in the same way as head-scarves were worn in the Second World War. Often the female slave children wear shabby cotton dresses and their hair is braided at various parts of the head; the braids are tied with roughly torn strips of cotton rag. Male slave children would wear shabby trousers or shorts, torn shirts and ragged straw hats.

CHAPTER SEVEN

ECCLESIASTICAL

This is a highly specialized field, and I have no doubt that I shall in my ignorance perpetrate appalling heresies. The guidance offered is very general, and again, the wardrobe mistress keeps her fingers crossed in the pious hope that her audience is not too knowledgeable and carping.

Much detailed information is contained in the late Nevil Truman's *Historic Costuming*; also, the illustrations in *The Pictorial Encyclopaedia of Fashion* will be found of great assistance in the matter of fabric design. For those resident in London, there is always the Victoria and Albert Museum; for accurate information regarding meticulous detail as to colour, special festivals etc., the expert will, of course, be the local incumbents.

The *cassock* is a plain, instep-length coat, with plain sleeves. It can be cut from the same pattern as the American Civil War uniform, lengthening the skirt.

The *alb* is a full-length white tunic, with long, loose sleeves. Use a man's shirt pattern; cut the yoke as given, and make the back and front sections about double the width. Gather the surplus into the yoke at back and front. Open at the back, sufficiently to slip over the head, and tie with tapes. Cut the sleeve from the same pattern, but do not slant in to the wrist.

Figure 97 Chasuble

The *chasuble* is roughly an ellipse, with a central hole for the head. It is usually decorated with 'orphreys', which are Y-shaped contrasting bands back and front, and round the outer edge. Variations in shape and width occur over the years, but the basic construction is the same. The average width at the shoulders is from elbow to elbow, and the length just below the calf. Cut as indicated in *figure 97*, in one piece if possible, and line. Silk or brocatelle is suitable for the chasuble, with contrasting orphreys. Rayon or similar material can be used for lining.

113

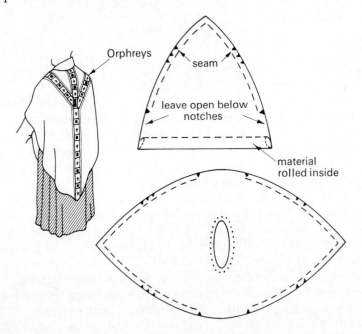

Orphreys

seam

leave open below notches

material rolled inside

Figure 97   Chasuble, with diagram

Attach the orphreys before inserting the lining. The latter undertaking has a trap for the unwary, and most of us have fallen into it at some time or another. You *can't* just put the two pieces together and machine round the neck and round the outer edge, because if you do, it's impossible to turn it right side out. But since necks are always a nuisance, it is worth doing the neck first. Mark out the correct position on the wrong side of the lining, but don't cut, and don't cut the main section. Lay the two sections together, right sides inside, pin at intervals to stop slipping; baste together round marked neckline, machine, and then cut away the neck opening. Snip the edges all round so that they lie flat when the lining is pulled through the opening. Before pulling the lining through the neck opening, make a series of matching notches as indicated on diagram, similar to those on a printed pattern.

Pull lining through at neck, press and run a row of machine stitching $\frac{1}{4}$ in ($\frac{1}{2}$ cm) from the edge.

Place flat on table, and starting at one pointed end, roll up the two thicknesses towards the neck; put in a few tying tacks to keep from unrolling. Fold back the two other ends, bringing the right sides together and matching the points and notches. The rolled section is now inside. Machine together between the points indicated on the diagram. Trim and snip turnings so that they lie flat on the curves; work the rolled piece through to right side—it will slide through the unmachined gap from the fold. Release the roll, and then roll up the section already machined, and tack as before. Fold back the raw edges again, and machine as before, leaving sufficient space to work the roll through the gap to the right side. It is only necessary to leave the gap one side, so the second machining can begin where the first one left off. Turn right side out, and close gap by slip-stitching lining to main fabric. This will be quite a short stretch, on the straight of the fabric. This may sound a complicated operation, but it saves the chore of turning in two curved edges and sewing them together by hand.

Alternatively, if it is necessary to make the chasuble in two sections, due to limitation in fabric width, the insertion of the lining is correspondingly easier. Cut the two sections of main fabric and of lining (the seams may either be centre back/front, or on the shoulders). Deal with each section in turn, before joining up. Place lining on main fabric, right sides inside; baste together at neck edge and on curved edge, leaving the straight edges open. Machine together, snip on curves and pull through at the straight edges. *Note* Leave about $\frac{5}{8}$ in ($1\cdot5$ cm) free at the beginning and end of each seam.

Place the two sections together, right sides inside, and machine together the main fabric but not the lining. Press open seams of main fabric, turn in one edge of lining, tuck the other raw edge underneath and slip-stitch straight edges of lining into place.

Figure 98   Cope and mitre

The *cope* is much simpler to make. It is a semi-circle of fabric having a radius slightly longer than the wearer's neck-to-floor measurement. It is as well to choose material with a firm weave, to eliminate the tendency to drop on the bias edges. If this seems likely, flatten the curve slightly when cutting.

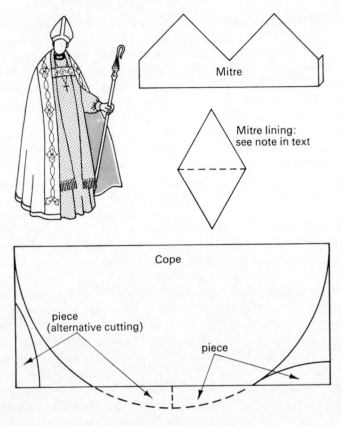

Mitre

Mitre lining:
see note in text

Cope

piece
(alternative cutting)

piece

Figure 98   Cope and mitre, with diagram

It is unlikely that the material will be wide enough to cut the whole cope in one piece (for an adult, at any rate), and it will be necessary to piece it as indicated in *figure 98*. The piecings can come out of the discards, as shown. Join the short edges first. then join to main cope. This will probably be on the selvedge, which should be snipped to prevent pucker.

Make the lining in the same way, and place the two pieces together, right sides inside. Machine all round, as indicated by black line, leaving the straight edge open enough to turn the cope through. Close gap as for chasuble. Press carefully, pushing the lining away from the edge. Set a row of pins all round about 6 in (15 cm) from the edge, and make invisible tie-tacks at intervals, particularly on the bias lines, to stop the lining from dropping.

Trim with contrasting bands, and attach a matching band across the chest, to fasten cope in place.

The *mitre* is cut as in *figure 98*, the foundation of buckram, covered with the same material as the cope. Decorate as required, and follow the same method of making as described for other headdresses with a buckram foundation. The lining is diamond shaped. The sides are the same length as the edges of the mitre, but the angle of the points is slightly more acute, making the points of the mitre curve to the shape of the head. The lateral diagonal of this piece will be about 2 in (5 cm) less than the head measurement halved. Press the turning allowance inwards and slip-stitch to the straight edges of the mitre.

Steam carefully to a slightly oval shape, to fit head, and tilt the points inwards. This will pull the sides inwards a little to give the outward slant of the sides. A loop of double thread linking the points about 2 in (5 cm) apart will help to maintain this slant and will not show at a distance.

At the back, the mitre has two narrow streamers, decorated and fringed.

A small inner cap will stop the mitre from dropping too low over the forehead. This need only be a straight piece of white cotton or the like, the length of the head measurement and about 5 in (13 cm) wide. Hem one long side; thread a tape through the hem; join short side; turn in seam allowance and slip-stitch into place round lower edge of mitre. Draw in to fit with tape, and tie.

Gowns, surplices, cottas dalmatics, etc., can be cut from the basic Plantagenet pattern, with suitable modification as to length, width of sleeve etc. Stoles, amices, and maniples are straight pieces of material of various sizes and are shown and described clearly in Truman. The same applies to monastic garb.

Figure 99   Square cap, biretta and skull cap

Unless rigid authenticity is required, the cap described in the chapter on Accessories may be worn, or the *square cap* shown in the figure. Cut this as indicated in the diagram. It can be made from felt, which is easiest to handle; or from facecloth, gaberdine, hopsack, dress cloth, or velvet. If the felt is thick enough, it will hold its shape without lining, and a wide-brimmed black felt hat could be cut up. The fine felt such as is sold for making toys will need an interlining of Vilene; so will cloth or velvet.

Cut the cap and the interlining from the same pattern, match up and machine seams in one operation. Make a silk lining and slip-stitch into place. Join the quarters two-and-two, then join the two half-sections together.

From a cap of this sort the *biretta* developed (*figure 99*). The three seams were pinched up into ridges, the seam without a ridge being worn to the left. Make a pattern from newspaper as follows:

Fold a sheet in half. Mark the fold at 4 in (10 cm) and again at $8\frac{1}{2}$ in (20 cm). Mark bottom edges at 3 in (7·5 cm). At the 4 in (10 cm) point on the fold draw a line at right angles, 4 in (10 cm). Join the end of this line to the $8\frac{1}{2}$ in (20 cm) mark. From this point draw an upward curve to the top point, and a shallow down-curving line to the 3 in (7·5 cm) mark at lower edge. Cut along the curved lines; crease outwards at line a–b and inwards at line b–c. Cut four pieces. Join right front and right back together on lines a–a^i–b–d and machine a straight line on the right side at a–b. With the remaining two sections (left front, left back), trim away the curve a–a^i–b; join the straight line a–b and the curve b–d. Join the two halves together, on the lines d–b–a^i–a–a^i–b–d, that is, from front to back over crown.

As previously mentioned, felt is one of the most suitable materials for this cap, and if it is used it does not matter if the seams are on the outside, closely trimmed. Fine felt needs to be interlined, but the seam allowance of the interlining should be trimmed very close to the stitching so that the white edges do not show lines (if they do, dab with black paint or ink). Finish off with a lining as previously. This set of measurements should fit an average 22 in head, but the appropriate adjustments can always be made. The starting point is the base line to d which is one eighth the head measurement plus turning allowance.

Skull caps are sometimes needed, and a pattern can be cut as in *figure 99*. Take the head measurement and divide by four;

measure across crown to tops of ears and divide by two. Use these dimensions as indicated in diagram, erring on the small side—these caps should barely cover the crown of the head.

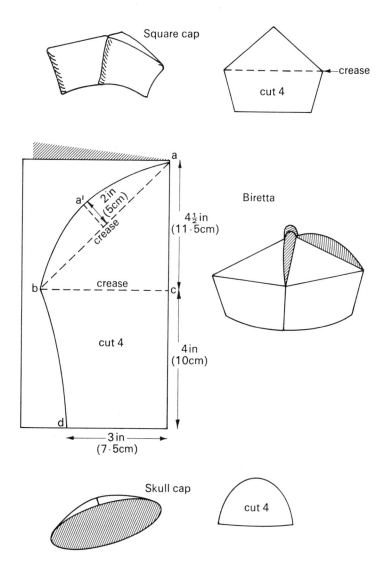

Figure 99   Square cap, biretta and skull cap, with diagrams

CHAPTER EIGHT

ACCESSORIES

This is another chapter of bits and pieces which it is hoped will come in useful from time to time. It is by no means exhaustive, and what has had to be omitted would fill another book. But all these ideas merely provide a starting point that will, I hope, trigger off further inspirations. The life of the wardrobe mistress is one of continual improvisation, and the most unlikely things will often achieve the desired effect. Even the professional world does not disdain this approach, and the highly effective costumes in the series 'The Six Wives of Henry the Eighth' made use of the most homely items which at a distance gave no indication of their humble origin.

Inspired serendipity features largely in this field, and by the time I had worked out this chapter, I had a shoe box full of the oddest assortment of what was virtually rubbish, converted into aglets, beads, medallions, fringe, etc. Everything used is easily obtainable, and expendable.

Figure 100   Stephane (diadem)

Use buckram to make the crescent-shaped diadem (or stephane) worn by Greek and Roman ladies. To cut pattern, fold a piece of paper, mark 6 in (15 cm) along bottom edge and 6 in along fold; draw a curved line between these two points. Mark ⅝ in (1·5 cm) beyond bottom of curve, and 3 in–4 in (8–10 cm) from first mark on fold. Draw a curve between these two marks. Buckram will obstinately roll up and resist all attempts to pin pattern to it unless tacked to a drawing board or the kitchen table. Anchor the pattern with drawing pins, weight it with books, or steam it flat. Stick on pattern at intervals with Scotch Tape. The pattern will fall away as you cut. (*Note*   It is worthwhile making a template of this pattern of thin card, as from it can also be made the French hood worn in the Tudor period. Also, it is easier to draw round a template with a ball-point pen, then cut the buckram.)

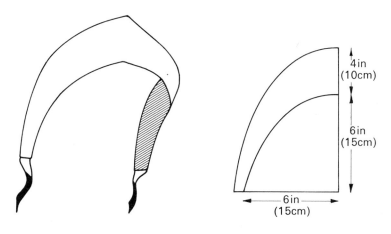

Figure 100   Stephane diadem

A useful piece of equipment for making this type of pattern is a 12 in (30 cm) flexible curve, from any shop selling drawing equipment.

The buckram can be gilded, silvered, covered with cooking foil, copper foil, or with fabric. If the latter, cut one piece of fabric the same size as the buckram and paint the edges with clear nail-varnish to prevent fraying. Cut another piece allowing $\frac{5}{8}$ in (1·5 cm) turnings all round. Carefully clip all curved edges about $\frac{1}{2}$ in (1 cm) inwards at 1 in (2·5 cm) intervals. Lay your material face downwards, and fit the buckram on top (a thin dab of Copydex here and there will stop it shifting). Copydex the edges all round, and fold turnings inwards, pressing down firmly. Copydex the smaller piece over the stuck-down edges. Cover a plastic 'Alice' band with ribbon or tape, and sew diadem firmly to it. ('Alice' bands are most useful properties, as so many headdresses can be attached to them— for example, the fontange of William and Mary period. They are now available already covered and padded.)

Figure 101   Armlets

I cannot find in the reference books any definite indication that the armlets so often seen in stage productions were, in fact, actually worn in Greek and Roman times. But as designers

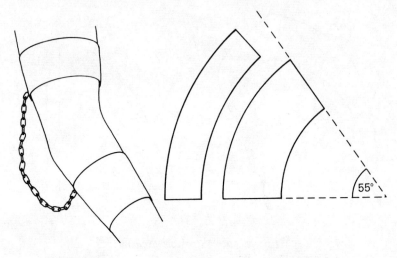

Figure 101 Armlets

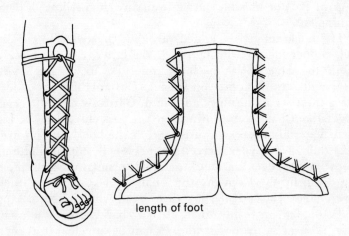

length of foot

Figure 102 Buskins

tend to use them for 'added interest', it seems worth while to
include them.

Painted or gilded buckram makes a good foundation and
there is now on the market a wide range of bonded vinyl
fabrics, self-stick metallic vinyls etc. These are not cheap, but
as these props can be used over and over again, they are useful

stock items, and a little extra expenditure is justified. Linking chain can be bought at most handicraft shops; this can be joined up and used again, as the links are sufficiently pliable to be opened and closed with pliers.

The same method as described for the stephane can be used to make the armlets. Cut from the cuff pattern in the basics (*figure 101*), and if using the buckram on its own, line it with flannel or winceyette, to prevent scratching. Attach this with Copydex. The bottom measurement will be $\frac{1}{2} \times$ (wrist measurement$+$1 in (2·5 cm)); the depth will vary according to choice and length of forearm; the top curve will correspond to the measurement round forearm, plus 1 in (2·5 cm) for overlap and fastening (large strong press-studs). The extra work entailed in making these armlets with fastenings is worth while because they can then be stored flat, without crushing.

Sandals

The wide variety of sandals now available disposes of the problem of footwear, though the choice should be made carefully, bearing in mind that the present-day 'slap-slap' becomes an irritating distraction on the stage.

Figure 102   Buskins

The buskin type of boot which may be needed for wear with a short Greek or Roman tunic can be made from felt or hessian. Felt should be lined with strong cotton; hessian may either be used double, or lined with cotton fabric. Cut as shown.

If using felt, the lining can be attached with two rows of close machine stitching, and the raw edges painted with colourless nail-varnish. If a swing-needle machine is available, use a 2·5 mm setting on a short stitch length.

Attach to a purchased sole, using double-glazed thread. Pierce fronts with stiletto or skewer at 3 in (7 cm) intervals, $\frac{3}{4}$ in (2 cm) from edge, and thread with cord or long boot-laces.

Hessian, although cheaper, requires more work. Because hessian frays, the inner and outer boot must be machined together on three edges, leaving open the bottom edge, which should be the selvedge. Turn right side out, press thoroughly, and run another row of machine stitching all round—including bottom edge, so that lining is firmly attached, before stitching to sole. As hessian dyes very well, any suitable colour may be obtained. Make boots first, and dye before attaching sole.

Figure 103   Aiguillettes

These were Shakespeare's 'aglet-babies'—ornamental metal tags which made it possible to thread the points or cords which held garments together.

They can be made from the tops of yoghurt or cream pots to about 3 in (8 cm) in diameter. Wash and smooth out carefully with a knife handle. Roll firmly round a pencil until the coil holds its tubular shape, then open it up carefully until it will slide over the tip of the little finger. Stroke gently with a twisting action until the foil forms a cone. The slight spring in the foil will hold its shape without adhesive, and although the 'aglet' will not stand up to rough usage, it will serve where the points are only decorative and not actually used to thread through the garment. These cost nothing to renew. Smaller 'aglets' can be made from milk-bottle tops; if these are smoothed carefully, the inward curve is gradually eliminated.

Push the end of the cord or ribbon into the 'aglet' and sew with fairly large stitches, taking care not to tear the foil with the thread.

If a more ornamental aglet is required, it can be made from a cone of buckram, painted and trimmed with braid or galon. Aglets were used on ribbon ties to fasten robes together, and a portrait of a Spanish queen by Sanchez Coello shows these ties clearly. They are all tied in a half-bow, so that the aglets hang level, and form an attractive decoration. There is a knack in tying the half-bow and getting the tags even: the ribbons are of uneven lengths, the right hand ribbon being about half the length of the left hand one. Start as if you were tying a reef knot. Pass left over right, pull through and tighten. Now bring the left back to right but do not loop it. Loop right, pass it over left, then under, and pull through. Adjust so that aglets hang even, and the loop stands upright.

More substantial aglets can also be made from rolled paper, and the same method can be used for making beads. This

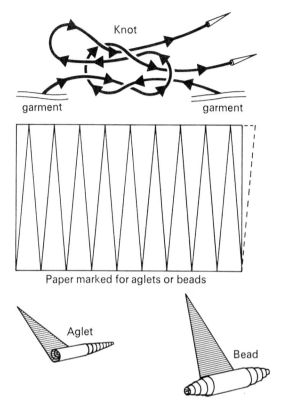

Figure 103 'Aiguillettes'

method evolved from a do-it-yourself craze which sprang up during the 1914–1918 War. I can remember assiduously cutting, rolling and colouring with crayon, and coloured wall-paper was also much in demand. For small beads or aglets, cigarette papers serve; the longer the paper, the fatter the bead.

Cut the paper as indicated in the diagrams. For an aglet, keep one side straight; for a bead, cut an isosceles triangle. It is easier and less wasteful in the latter case to cut a thin cardboard template. It is then quite simple to measure out a parallelo-gram slightly longer than the template, and mark out the first triangle with one long side to the straight edge of the paper. Mark the resulting base angle, reverse the template and fit one long side to the diagonal, mark the other base angle, and so on.

A whole sheet of coloured paper can be marked out in this way, and time will be saved.

Cut the triangles exactly, and starting at the base, carefully roll the strip round a fine knitting needle. For the aglets it will be necessary from time to time to slide the strip off the needle and knock one edge straight. The beads must roll evenly up the middle, to keep them symmetrical. Secure the point with adhesive or a sliver of Scotch Tape. These beads, of course, would be particularly in keeping with a play set in about 1915.

Figure 104   Moccasins

To make a pattern, trace the wearer's foot on paper and cut a sole. (Round off at the toe, as moccasins have no left and right.) Place this sole on a larger piece of paper, positioning it about 3 in (7·5 cm) from the side edge, and the same distance from the bottom edge. Mark the curve of the heel and from this drop a straight line to the edge of the paper. From the edge of the sole pattern, mark out all round, about 2 in (5 cm). This gives a rough pattern allowing scope for adjustment, according to the thickness of the wearer's foot. Trim away the M-shaped piece at the heel.

To make the toe piece, draw a line across the sole pattern just past the widest part of the foot, towards the heel. Match this line with the edge of the paper, trace round and cut accordingly.

Join back of heel a–b to e–f so that it fits snugly on to curve of heel. (The lines b–c and d–e each equal half the curve c–d.) Stitch straight edge to curve c–d. The measurement at a–b (e–f) will probably be rather deeper than the average shoe heel, as will the edges a–g and f–h, but this does not matter, as they can be rolled back to form a cuff.

It will probably be necessary to trim away on the outer curve g–h, but before doing so, try on for size. Slide the foot firmly into the heel and stand on the sole, pulling slightly under the foot—it is no use making these moccasins sloppy. Lay upper section in place on top of foot and pin to fit at the instep, matching i–l and k–n. (If necessary, a slit can be left at these points and tied with a thong, if it seems that the wearer will have difficulty in getting shoe on.) Pin and adjust at the toe and at intervals round the curve l–m–n. Detach carefully from the

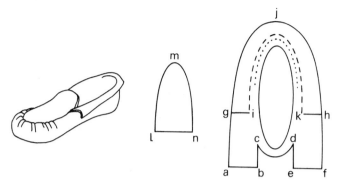

Figure 104   Moccasins

upper by disengaging the pins, but still leaving them through the sole piece, to act as a guide. Run a strong gathering thread along this line and draw up to fit upper. Fasten off the gathering thread firmly, then stitch firmly to upper. Trim away the surplus round the front, and leave the back surplus to form a cuff.

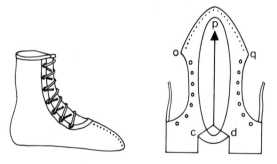

Figure 105   Mediaeval footwear

Figure 105   Mediaeval footwear

The same method can be used for making soft slipper-type footwear. By dispensing with the curved upper and cutting the sole piece as in *figure 105*, a rough sandal emerges, suitable for peasants and serving men. Cut out the V-shaped piece, making the measurement c/d–p equal to that from heel to toe. Fold point o to point q and join seam. The measurement o–q should be taken round the foot at its widest point. Make eyelet holes as marked, and lace together.

These shoes will be more substantial if a bought insole is machined on the inside before the sewing operation is begun. Match the sole to the heel curve c–d, fix with Copydex and tack in place—machine it, if the machine will take it, though cork would tend to crumble. For extra strength an outer sole can be added. Fix this in the same way, with Copydex, then stitch into place with stab stitches. Then make up as above.

Figure 106   Tudor slipper

Further variations in cutting are shown at *figure 106* for making the soft slippers which can be copied from pictures in the costume books.

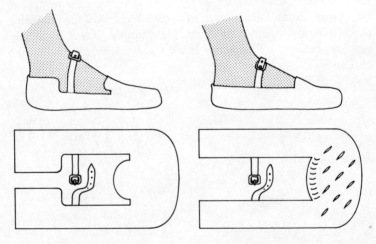

Figure 106   Tudor slipper

Figure 107   Shoe with long pointed toe

In the fourteenth and fifteenth centuries, the toes of shoes were very pointed—usually they had to be padded, and in extreme instances, looped up to the top of the bootee with a chain. Such exaggerations are for the most part best avoided unless a considerable amount of practice in wearing is put in. Otherwise, pointed-toed slippers can be made either on moccasin lines, with or without outer soles, or they can be made by cutting just the

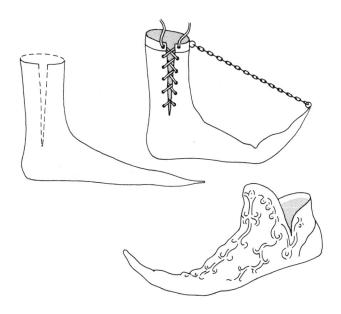

Figure 107   Shoe with long pointed toe

uppers and stitching to soft bedroom slippers. A small curved upholstery needle will be necessary for this operation.

Figure 107 shows the cut of the long pointed toes, which can be stuffed with old nylons.

It is not practicable to go much further than the Elizabethan period in the matter of do-it-yourself footwear, on account of the introduction of solid heels. For authoritative guidance on shoe styles, you cannot do better than consult Eunice Wilson's fascinating and comprehensive *History of Shoe Fashions*.

As regards materials, practically any closely woven fabric can be used. Velvet, satin, felt, hessian, leather, suède, vinyls etc., depending upon the degree of durability required. The first four will, of course, require to be lined with a firm material, e.g. cotton or winceyette.

Figures 108 and 109   Tudor cap

This cap, which is a development of the 'barret' (or biretta, or beret) type, is useful for a very wide range of characters such as old men, tutors, clergy, magistrates etc., and Portia (*Merchant of Venice*).

Black or scarlet cloth, velvet, or felt can be used. Felt is obviously the most convenient, as it needs less finishing off. Very thin felt will need to be used double, possibly with an interlining. These sections can be fused together with dabs of Copydex, and a row of machining round the edge. Join the back seam by overlapping rather than placing the edges together.

The top of the crown is circular or slightly oval, having a circumference equal to the head measurement of the wearer.

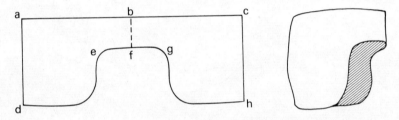

Figure 108   Early Tudor cap, with diagram

The diameter of this circle is roughly one-third of that measurement. Fold a piece of newspaper into four. Mark from the folded point $\frac{1}{2} \times \frac{1}{3}$ head measurement. For example: head measurement 21 in (53·5 cm) divided by 3 = 7 in (8 cm) halved = $3\frac{1}{2}$ in (9 cm). *Mark* (not cut) a circle on the folded paper and on the folded edge make another mark about $\frac{1}{2}$ in (1 cm) beyond the first mark. This slightly oblate shape will give a better fit than a true circle (as any ex-matelot will tell you). Cut the main section 2 in (5 cm) longer than the head measurement, to allow for overlap. a–c = the head measurement. a–d and c–h = height from point of jaw to crown of head (roughly one-third a–c). b–f = $\frac{1}{3}$ × a–d. e–g = a–d + 1 in (2·5 cm) for an adult, slightly less for a small child. *Figure 108* gives the basic template with average measurements. (Head sizes seem to vary between 21 and 23 in, and adjustment can be made accordingly.) It is capable of considerable variation.

In its simplest form it can be made in vinyl, to serve as a soldier's helmet. (It may not be particularly authentic, but it will blend in well with the trend for somewhat stylized costumes which although not specifically identifiable, nevertheless do give a sense of period. I am aware that to the purists, this is heresy, but once the curtain has gone up, it works, and only the most carping audience would complain.)

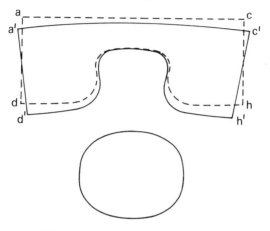

Figure 109   Variation on Fig. 108

Figure 109 shows a minor modification suggested to turn it into Portia's cap in the trial scene. Pivot the lines a–d and c–h as indicated by heavy lines. This brings the side pieces closer to the cheeks and tucks the back seam closer into the nape of the neck. It also widens the crown laterally and shortens it from back to front, so the crown must be modified accordingly. Make up the cap first, fit on the wearer, and check the variation necessary in the crown, which will be slightly more elliptical.

Figure 110   Hennins

Carried out in more exotic materials, with added decoration, the basic template used for *figure 108* can be adapted to make a mediaeval headdress. A becoming variation is to omit the crown, take a long scarf in some soft flowing material, pass it under the chin, thread the ends upwards through the cap, and allow them to fall down the back.

By bending the lines a–c and a–d/c–h into curves, as in *figure 110*, indicated again by heavy lines, the cap is converted

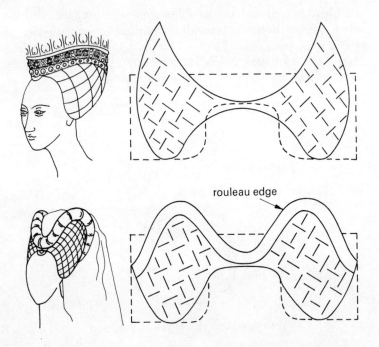

rouleau edge

Figure 110   Hennins, with diagram

into a headdress of the later Plantagenet era. Cover in rich material, and give a reticulated impression with criss-crossed braid or cord. Fill in the top with soft, dark material. It can be finished either to produce a coronet effect, such as appears in a portrait of Margaret of Denmark, Queen of Scotland (attributed to Hugo van der Goes, 1476), or the cap can dip steeply to the forehead, and be edged with a contrasting rouleau, cut on the bias, seamed into a thin tube and stuffed with old nylons.

By curving downwards to centre back, the heart-shaped line is achieved. The crown filling can be omitted, and a flowing veil attached centre front and at the side points, to hang down the back.

Figure 111   'Dogberry' cap

With further exaggeration the cap moves into the near-grotesque.

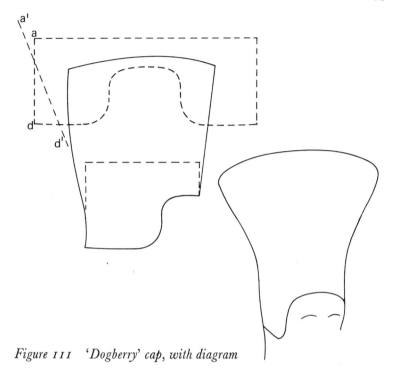

Figure 111 '*Dogberry' cap, with diagram*

By projecting the line a^i–d^i considerably higher, a fantastic hat emerges fit for Dogberry at his most portentous.

The actual making up of the headgear follows the lines already explained. The foundation can be of buckram or, for the women's headdresses, of esparterie (some milliners call it 'spartra') as this is lighter and easier to handle. The hennin caps will look better if lightly padded. Much use can be made of sticking and tacking, unless the finished article is required to last for a long time.

Figure 112   Soft calash

The calash was a hood for outdoor wear fashionable in the 1770s. Its shape derived from the calêche, a carriage with a folding top. It was at its most exaggerated in the period of towering headdresses, and it was necessary to stiffen it with

Figure 112   Soft calash

hoops of whalebone.* However, a similar hood on a much smaller scale is often useful—I have seen one used in a Sheridan production—and this can be made on the same lines as the sunbonnet described in the American chapter.

The method of piping is the same, but the front brim is cut down to about 1½ in (4 cm) and the neck frill to 2 in (5 cm). A simpler method of making, which in fact appears in some of the surviving examples, is to dispense with the shaped back panel and cut the main section about 3 in (8 cm) wider. Carry through the piping operation as before, then fold in half and seam up the centre back from neck edge to within 3 in (8 cm) of the top fold. Working from the inside, gather round this open edge, draw tight and fasten off. Trim on the outside with a matching bow.

The most suitable material for this scaled-down calash is a soft satin, silk, or rayon. It is more convenient in wear and less of an embarrassment than the large one, as by loosening the strings, the wearer can simply let it fall back on the shoulders.

Figure 113   Plain bonnets

Nowadays bonnets are worn only by the very young, but in earlier days they were worn indoors, and even in bed, by the middle-aged and elderly. Many examples still remain in costume museums, and even the plainest and most humble bonnet often displays the most exquisite handiwork, being

---

* Detailed instructions for making this structure are given in *Stage Costumes and How to Make Them.*

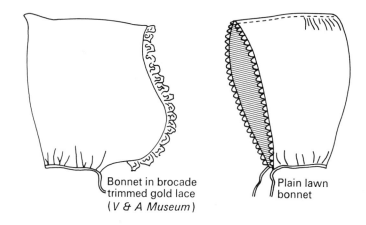

Bonnet in brocade
trimmed gold lace
(*V & A Museum*)

Plain lawn
bonnet

Figure 113   Plain bonnets

closely embroidered and edged with lace.

The pattern is elementary—a straight strip of material, mostly white lawn or cotton, shaped to the head in various ways. Two measurements are necessary: A. over the head from just below the ears; B. round the back of the head from the corners of the eyes.

If a bonnet with a back seam is required, the length of the strip will be 'A' and the width $\frac{1}{2} \times$ 'B'. The crown can be left as a 'poke', or gathered and drawn downwards in the manner described for making the back of the calash.

Quite a number of existing examples, however, have the seam at the top, and the gatherings are therefore drawn towards the front. Some of them are shaped slightly to a curve over the forehead and cheeks. In each case the lower edge is finished off with a hem through which a tape is threaded, to tie under the chin.

All the more elaborate forms of headdress, such as 'hennins', 'gables', French hoods and so on, disappeared when Elizabeth I tossed hers away and rode to her coronation with her red–gold hair flowing over her shoulders, and for about a hundred years no one, except servants and Puritans, wore caps. In the 1690s they seem to have reappeared as an item of fashion, and hung on, in various forms, for another two-hundred years, although latterly it was only the elderly who clung to them. Since then there have been a couple of rather 'gimmicky' reincarnations: 'Juliet' caps for evening wear in about 1912, and 'Boudoir' caps, the latter for ladies who had the leisure to sit around in boudoir gowns (something a little more elaborate than a dressing-gown). I can remember this type of cap as late as 1915, though it was rather an affectation by then.

Figure 114   *Fontange*

One of the most elaborate forms of cap ever worn was the fontange, which probably came to this country with Mary II

Figure 114   *Fontange*

and Dutch William. The easiest way to make it is to attach graduated frills to an 'Alice' band. Cut two strips of net or lace 18 in (46 cm) × 11 in (28 cm). Position piece 2 on top of piece 1, 1¾ in (4·5 cm) below the top (long) edge. Measure 8 in (20 cm) from the top of piece 1 (lower piece). Fold and pin along this line, and then gather securely. Draw up until the gathers fit across the crown of the head (about 6 in/15 cm) and sew firmly to a padded 'Alice' band. Pull all four frills upright, and put a few holding stitches through the pleats near the band, to keep them from falling away. If using a bordered curtain net, it is necessary to cut four separate frills graduated in the same proportions. In that case, match together the two long un-bordered edges of the two narrowest pieces, with the narrower of the two underneath. Match together the long unbordered edges of the other two pieces, with the narrower piece on top. Lap these edges over the edges of the other two pieces, pin, then gather as before. This is better than gathering all four un-bordered edges, which would create a problem in keeping the frills upright. By doing it as described, the two sets will pull against each other and eliminate the tendency to flop forward.

Finish off the fontange with a circle of net or lace gathered into a tiny mob cap to cover the back of the head. Attach about one quarter of this to the band and secure in place in wear with hair grips.

Trim each side with loops of ribbon and a streamer of narrow lace.

Alternatively, pleated frilling of varied widths can be used. This is rather expensive and not always easy to find in the shops but it does save trouble.

Figure 115 Mob cap

No intricate cutting is involved here, as the mob cap is simply a circle drawn up to fit the head of the wearer. The size can vary as required. The size of the brim depends on the placing of the casing to carry the gathering tape—the farther from the edge, the wider the frill. Some of these caps were hardly more than a token, sitting on the crown or the back of the head, decorated with frills, ribbons and streamers. The serving maid would wear a larger one, in plain cotton or lawn. If her place in the serving hierarchy were slightly more elevated, she might be permitted an unpretentious narrow lace edge.

At times the mob cap reached considerable proportions, notably to accommodate the mass of curls fashionable just before the French Revolution. To avoid expenditure of material on an enormous circle, there is a more economical way of achieving the same effect. The brim section can be made from a straight piece, attached to the circumference of the main circle. Join the straight piece to the circle, taking a turning

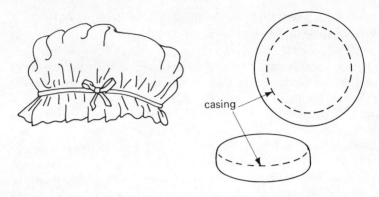

Figure 115   Mob cap

sufficient to carry the drawing tape. Machine the straight edge
back on to the circle, to form a casing. Do this with the straight
edge on top, easing in the underneath surplus. (The small
puckers disappear when the cap is drawn up to fit.) This
method can be used if a cap with a plain crown and lace brim is
required. Many seventeenth and eighteenth-century portraits
show these small caps worn under hats, a fashion which survives
in the picturesque Welsh national costume.

Below stairs, caps and bonnets persisted long after the lady of
the house had discarded hers.

The variety of caps and bonnets in this field would fill a
book on their own. I can only describe one or two ideas.

Figure 116   Victorian maid's cap

The figure shows a basic cap copied from one in the Victoria
and Albert Museum. It is capable of considerable variation.
Take a piece of paper 6 in (15 cm) × 24 in (61 cm) and fold
the two short edges together. With the fold to the right, make
two marks on the fold, the first 3¾ in (9·5 cm) (f) and the second
5¾ in (4·5 cm) (c) from the bottom right hand corner. Make
another mark along the bottom edge 8 in (20 cm) (e) from right
hand corner. Mark 3 in (7·5 cm) (d) up left hand edge, and
from this point mark point (a) 1½ in (2·5 cm) above point (d).
Draw the short line a–b = ¾ in (2 cm) at right angles to the

edge, and join points b–d. With gently curved lines, join b–c, d–e and e–f. These are the main cutting lines. Open out the resulting pattern. b–d is the centre back seam; e–f is the front, framing the face; d–e fits round the neck, and strings are attached at point (e). This diagram does not include turnings, so when cutting, the appropriate allowance should be made— ½ in (1 cm) turnings are sufficient, as they are trimmed away after seaming, to avoid ridges. The secret of a good fit here is that this section is cut on the bias. Fold back a triangle of the fabric and position the pattern with the line a–c close to the diagonal fold. This leaves the maximum for the crown, which is

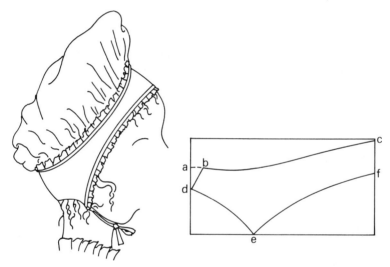

Figure 116   Victorian maid's cap, with diagram

circular, and can vary considerably. If a small, close-fitting cap is required, cut the circle with a diameter only slightly larger than is necessary to cover the back of the head when this section is fitted. The larger the circle, the fuller the crown will be, and variations in style emerge merely from altering the setting of the gathers. If instead of a true circle, an ovoid piece is cut, setting the narrow end to the back and concentrating the gathers closely across the crown, a rather Dickensian effect is obtained. A circle of 16–20 in (40–50 cm) is a workable minimum.

The circle is cut single; the fitted section is double. To

assemble, first join the back seams b–d of both pieces. Try for size, as this cap needs to fit snugly over the ears and round the head. It is easier to fit the circle by means of pinch pleats, and the effect is better than gathers. Set a pin each end of the diameter, for centre back and centre front. Make about 10 pinch pleats each side of centre front, about 1 in (2·5 cm), each meeting the fold of the previous one, without overlapping. Set the pleats so that the edges turn inwards to centre front. The pleats round the back can be smaller, set at wider intervals.

Baste pleats in position, then fit the other section over this section, so that the pleated circle is sandwiched in between. Machine firmly, preferably with a double line of stitches as there is considerable strain here. Take care not to stretch the bias, otherwise the fit will be spoiled.

From the remainder of the material cut narrow frills to finish off the face and neck edges. A narrow frill can be included at the circle edge, and this should be inserted and sandwiched with the circle. Alternatively, lace can be used as a finish.

This cap, of average size, can be made from 1 yd (1 m) of lawn, cotton, nylon etc.; if trimmed with lace, allow twice the combined measurement round neck and face, i.e. $2\frac{1}{2}$–2 yd (or metres). The measurements given will fit a 21 in head (23·5 cm).

Figure 117   Ruffs

The ruff evolved from the threading of a draw-string through the wide neck of the shirt. It was soon considerably elaborated, and Mary Tudor's marriage to the Spanish king established it firmly in this country.

The method of making a plain ruff is simple. It is a very long, straight piece of material, reduced by pleating to the neck measurement of the wearer. Tarlatan, stiffly starched lawn, organdie or any other very stiff material will serve. The larger the ruff, the fuller it must be, in order to create the wider circumference. Also, smaller pleats are better. Make sure that the material is dead straight, and free from creases. Before starting to pleat, mark both long edges at equal intervals. Mark the neck edge first, every 2 in (5 cm). This can be done with ink or pencil, as it will not show. The outer edge must be marked with a thread, and to get the final effect, this mark is half way between its opposite number. That is to say, at the neck edge, make the first mark 2 in (5 cm) from the corner, the second 4 in (10 cm) and so on. For the outer edge, take a needle with a long thread and pass it through the fabric at 1 in (2·5 cm), 3 in (7·5 cm) and so on, and gather into loose pleats, without creasing material. *Note* These conversions to metric are only approximate, so when taking these measurements, either one or the other must be adhered to and adjustments made accordingly. For instance, 1–3–5 in will become 3–8–13 cm and so on. Provided exactness is maintained, it is a matter of choice which is used. Metric often works out more exactly than Imperial.

When you have pleated sufficient strips to fill neck measurement, join the sections together by a very narrow overlap, making sure that this always comes at the centre (the 1–3–5 point) of a pleat.

Take a piece of ribbon velvet the same width as the pleat and long enough to fit neck measurement plus 1 in (2·5 cm). Neaten ends and make a fastening with a piece of 'Velcro', press-studs, hooks or tapes. Put the velvet surface to the inside; it will be more comfortable.

Crease with the fingernail along about 1 in (2·5 cm) of the width at each mark along the neck edge, and oversew the point of each crease to the velvet, about ¼ in (0·5 cm) apart. At the outer edge, draw up the gathering thread fairly tightly and knot the end to prevent slipping. Tie edges of the pleats together in alternating pairs, half-way between top and centre (see diagram) to achieve the figure-of-eight effect of the portraits. If this is done neatly, it will not show from a distance. The real thing was probably done with a 'goffering' iron (something like curling tongs), but you will no longer find one in the hardware store.

With regard to quantities, it is difficult to be precise. Somewhere there must be a formula for calculating the ratio of pleat to depth and circumference, and I have no doubt that in Elizabethan days a ruff maker could have told you to an inch how much material was required. All I can offer is a rule-of-thumb method of working it out. (Most wardrobe mistresses find things out for themselves the hard way, by a process of trial and error.) Take a strip of newspaper of the required

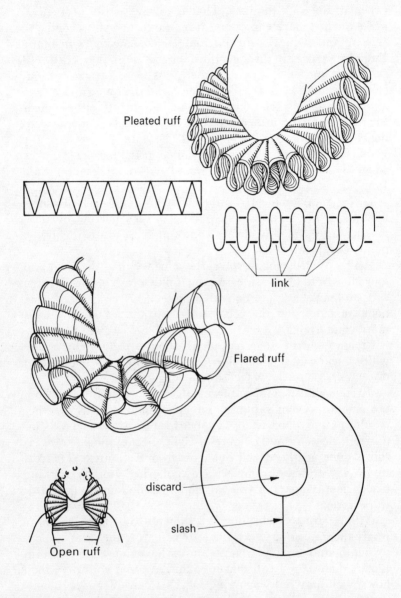

Pleated ruff

link

Flared ruff

discard

slash

Open ruff

Figure 117   Ruffs

depth, about a yard (or metre) long, and mark out on the 1–3–5–7 edge. Gather these points together carefully, without creasing the paper, and secure with a paper clip. Then with further paper clips, link the loops together as shown in diagram (starting from the right, link bottom left and top left of first loop to bottom right and top right of adjacent loop and so on). Remove the centre paper clip, and pull gently apart. Divide the circumference of the ruff by the resulting measurement to find out how many strips are required, and throw in an extra one to be on the safe side. (34 in will make 6 pleats each $2\frac{1}{2}$ in deep and expanding to about 6 in. 34 in is mentioned because this is the width of an average newspaper, which doesn't cost anything to cut up.)

To calculate the circumference of the ruff, use the following formula:

One third neck measurement plus twice depth of ruff.
Multiply this measurement by three.

For example, a ruff $2\frac{1}{2}$ in deep, having a $2\frac{1}{2}$ in pleat, to fit a 15 in neck:

$\frac{1}{3} \times 15 = 5+5 = 10 \times 3 = 30$ in circumference.

Allow 6 strips $2\frac{1}{2}$–3 in wide and 36 in long. The extra strip makes allowance for the slight variation, so that the ruff could be slightly deeper without looking skimped.

Rubens' portrait of himself and his wife Isabella, painted in 1610, shows this type of ruff, though considerably larger. But the method of calculation is the same. Isabella's ruff is edged with lace, and certainly makes the most attractive frame for her face. One can only regret that it would be necessary to travel to Munich to see the portrait. However, there are many other paintings of the period in which such ruffs appear, and they can also be seen in church monuments.

Another style of ruff fashionable in the early 1600s was fluted rather than pleated, and this gives it far more lightness in effect, without the stiffness of the mill-wheel ruff. The portrait of Magdalena Duchess of Neuberg, reproduced on the cover of James Laver's *Concise History of Costume* shows this style in some detail.

Instead of straight, pleated strips, this ruff seems to be composed of flares so full as to fall into soft pleats. This effect can be achieved by cutting three or even four complete circles of stiff net or organdie, cutting out the centre of each circle, slitting along the radius, and joining the straight edges. The outer edge is then tacked into flutes in the same way as the straight ruff, and the inner edge reduced, if necessary, by small box pleats to fit the neck measurement. The centre circle to be removed should have a circumference equal to about one third the neck measurement. This ruff looks attractive edged with lace, eased on to allow for the sweep of the circle, but this is rather extravagant. An economical method would be to use plastic lace table mats with the middles cut out in the manner described above. These will require stiffening, and should be mounted on Vilene, cut to the same pattern, but with a slightly smaller diameter, so that the patterned edge is left free, to give the illusion of lace. This method, incidentally, would be quite in keeping with the actual portrait, which shows an inner ruff, underneath the lace, having a delicately coloured border.

This method can also be used to make the open ruff which followed on. It will be necessary to remove a slightly larger circle; two complete circles, suitably cut, will be sufficient, and the middle to be removed should have a circumference equal to the measurement from the back of the neck to the lower neck edge of the gown.

Figure 118   Plain lace collar and 'underpropper'

After the ruff, a lace collar was fashionable, shaped as in the figure. It is a circle or ellipse, squared off in front, a hole in the centre for the neck, slit up the front. This also can be contrived from plastic lace, as can the matching cuffs.

Slightly less stiff, and more becoming, was the 'whisk' collar, which could be entirely of lace, or laced edged, or quite plain. The present-day coat collar is cut on much the same lines, and can therefore be used as a guide, choosing one which does not have an exaggerated point.

All the above will need support. They were worn over a structure known as an 'underpropper'. This can be contrived from galvanized wire, which is more malleable than millinery wire. Make a framework as in *figure 118*, leaving long wire 'tails' which are inserted into casings on the costume seams.

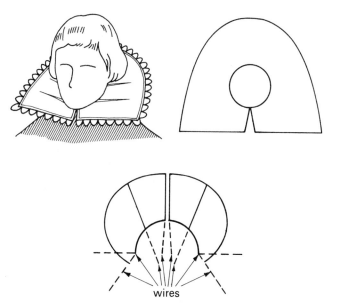

Figure 118   Plain lace collar and 'underpropper'

These 'tails' need to be about 5 in (12 cm) long. The ends must be bent back and bound with plaster, to prevent scratching. The main framework should be painted white, or bound with tape, ribbon, etc, to disguise it. The front two tails can be inset in a casing at the neck edge, the next two at the shoulder seam, two more midway between shoulder and centre back into casings along the lines of the back neck darts, and the centre back at the back seam. If the costume has no back fastening (as for instance, in a doublet, or a gown laced over a stomacher) one wire will be enough. For a gown with a back opening, the underpropper must be made in two sections, with casings either side. Tie the top points with narrow tape. If you are using a zipper, all you need to do is to machine the outer edge of the zipper tape, having tucked in and neatened the tops. This automatically forms a casing.

None of these collars is particularly comfortable to wear, but if the role calls for it, it must be endured. A certain stiffness of carriage is necessary, but this is not out of keeping with contemporary manners.

The more informal 'whisk' or 'falling band', became fashion-able later, particularly in the reign of Charles I, by which time much of the rigidity had disappeared from costume in general. As much lace as you can afford can be used, and reference to contemporary portraits will suggest a variety of styles. Even paper doilies can be used for a short-term costume.

Reticules, pouches, purses etc

Two explanations of the term 'reticule' exist. According to the dictionary, it signifies a 'small bag, originally and properly of *net*work, carried by ladies'. The other explanation is that it is a corruption of 'Ridicule', and there cannot be a woman who hasn't smarted under this adjective in reference to her handbag —and always from a man, the contents of whose pockets would probably fill half a dozen 'ridicules'.

Figure 119   Pouch

A small pouch slung from the belt is in keeping over a very wide period. All the fabrics and materials mentioned for shoes are suitable, and the degree of ornamentation is governed by the particular role. Belts and pouches afford great scope for decoration.

A simple pattern is shown at *figure 119*. When using soft fabrics, an interlining of buckram or double Vilene is necessary, and since these again are permanent, re-usable items, a little extra trouble is worth while.

Cut main fabric and lining with standard turnings, or if using buckram, mark out the same shape without allowing these turnings. Place main material wrong side up, position the buckram, lap over the turning allowance and secure with Copydex, taking care not to dab too near the edge, otherwise it makes the needle impossibly sticky. Iron down the turning allowance on the lining, and lay in place over the buckram. Baste round edges, then sew lining to main fabric with small slip-stitches on the extreme edge. These two sections can also be padded with a thin layer of wadding, although this is not absolutely necessary. At this stage carry out any decorating— braiding, beadwork, etc.—and also position the fastening. This

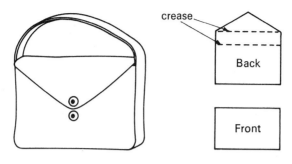

Figure 119   Pouch

can be a large press-stud gilded or painted so that it is not too obviously modern. Alternatively, the back-and-flap section can be tucked through a strap sewn to the front section. The strap is made as described below, reduced to about half the width.

The two sections are joined together by a soft gusset. Cut a strip of main fabric about $3\frac{1}{2}$ in (9 cm) wide, and also a strip of Vilene about $1\frac{1}{4}$ in (3 cm) wide. With wrong side upwards, lay the interfacing on top of the main strip, turn over and baste the seam allowance, fold the main strip in half, at the same time tucking in the seam allowance. Baste and machine, and also run a row of stitching on the fold side, about the width of the presser foot from fold.

The measurement of this 'strap' varies. If the pouch is to be worn slung from the shoulder, it must be of proportionate length. If it is to be hung from a belt, the actual pouch gusset must be just long enough to fit round the shaped edge of the front, plus a sufficient off-cut to make two sling loops which are sewn to the back of the pouch, big enough to take the belt. These could be attached before the final assembly of the pouch.

Lay front on the back section with lower edges matched, and mark top back edges with coloured threads. This makes it easier to get the gusset set in without 'wringing'. It also indicates the position of the loops. Crease the buckram along this line, and make a parallel crease towards the front, equal in width to the gusset. By matching the top edge of the front section to this second crease you can position the front fastening.

Finally, tuck in and neaten the cut edges of the loops and sew firmly to the back; join gusset first to the front section, then match top edges to the marked point on the back section, and stitch together, using small oversewing stitches.

This method can be used for any type of bag, of any period, varying the size as required. It is practically ageless and can be used from earliest times down to the present day.

Figure 120 '*Dorothy' bag and 'miser' purse*

Another reticule was the 'Dorothy' bag. This is perhaps the easiest of all to make, blends in with Regency, Victorian and Edwardian costume, and is frequently made of the same fabric as the gown. In its simplest form it is a straight piece of material with a broad hem and casing on each of the short sides, and the long sides folded in half and joined. Two loops of cord or ribbon are threaded through the casing and pulled to close the top. A variation of this is made from two circles (main and lining), with two machined rows of stitching to form a casing, about 2 in (5 cm) from the edge. Mark a diameter and work an eyelet hole each end; thread cords or ribbon and draw up to close. These bags are capable of enormous variety, both in size and in decoration. One pictured in a magazine of 1912 is criss-crossed with galon, embroidered with pearls, and the corners finished off with tassels.

Reticulated in its literal sense was the 'miser' or stocking purse, which was a long tube, closed and tasselled at each end, the centre of the seam being left open sufficiently to allow coins to be dropped in, and secured with two sliding rings. The purse was then looped through the belt. Purses of this type were apparently used in the main by men, and were often very beautiful in execution. They were obviously in use in Jane Austin's day, as is borne out by Charles Bingley's rather sarcastic comment regarding the accomplishments of young ladies, netting purses being amongst these. They also feature in a handbook of needlework published in 1842, which gives instructions for crocheted, knitted and netted purses, so one can assume that they were used until the mid-1800s. At one time I had a collection of about thirty and they displayed an astonishing variety—even the plainest had its steel tassel, sometimes faceted and pear-shaped, obviously purpose-made; sometimes

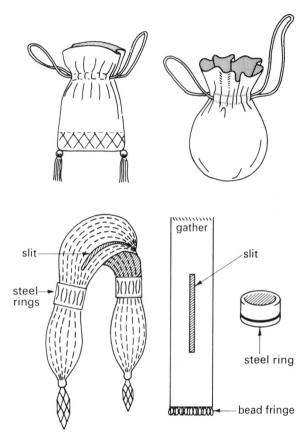

Figure 120 'Dorothy' bag and 'miser' purse

twisted strands of steel beads; sometimes steel-bead 'lace' or graduated loops and festoons.

To make the real thing would entail hours of intricate work, but with a little ingenuity they can be faked. Fine soft material is essential: curtain net, used double and dyed; silk velvet; Tricel jersey etc. Make a 'sausage' from a straight piece of material up to about 10 in (25 cm) long and 5 in (13 cm) wide. Join the long sides, leaving the centre 3 in (8 cm) open. Run a gathering thread at the ends, draw up and secure. Trim with a tassel. An ordinary silk tassel can be used, but a more authentic effect is obtained by making a tassel from small beads, fine chain loops, or even fishing weights covered with silver foil. It does seem that the beads actually used were always of steel, so a fairly dull effect must be aimed at, and gold beads would be quite out of keeping. An alternative method of finishing off was to gather one end with a tassel, and square off the other end, which was then ornamented with steel 'lace'. This effect can be achieved by linked bead loops.

The sliding rings are a little more of a problem—they were obviously purpose made and must be items which have long disappeared from the haberdashery counter. They were mostly about $\frac{5}{8}$ in (1 cm) wide and $\frac{3}{4}$ in (2 cm) in diameter, slightly waisted, and engraved or chased. On the thicker purses they are, of course, correspondingly larger. The obvious solution, if you can afford it, is stainless steel finger rings, otherwise, the ever useful buckram, covered with yoghurt tops (stronger than kitchen foil). Cut two pieces of buckram each 2 in (5 cm) × $\frac{5}{8}$ in (1 cm). Unwind about 3 in (7·5 cm) from a roll of Scotch Tape, and stick the strip to it. Wind round the finger till the ends of the buckram overlap slightly, then take a couple of turns of Scotch Tape to keep in place. Cut a strip from the smoothed-out yoghurt or cream top (they average 3 in (7·5 cm) in diameter) $1\frac{1}{4}$ in (3 cm) wide, and wind it round a pencil to induce spring. Wind it round the made ring, press the excess inwards and smooth down by inserting a pencil and pressing out all creases.

INDEX

Page numbers in italic refer to illustrations not shown on the same pages as the associated text.